CHANNELING

MY LIFE ON AIR, OFF AIR, AND IN LIVING COLOR

FRED HICKMAN

with

HARRISON GOLDEN

Published by Scorecard Press
Durham, North Carolina
ScorecardPress.com

Library of Congress Control Number: 2026902956

ISBN: 979-8-9943435-0-0 (hardcover)
ISBN: 979-8-9943435-1-7 (paperback)
ISBN: 979-8-9943435-2-4 (ebook)

First paperback edition 2026

10 9 8 7 6 5 4 3 2

TRIBUTES TO FRED HICKMAN

"A joy to work with and a joyful person."

— MICHAEL KAY, NEW YORK YANKEES
PLAY-BY-PLAY ANNOUNCER

"He was the first that allowed his ethnicity to show easily and comfortably."

— KENNY SMITH, TWO-TIME NBA CHAMP

"An excellent broadcaster whose legacy paved the way for Stuart Scott, Michael Wilbon, Stan Verrett, Steve Wyche, Jim Trotter, Jemele Hill, and others."

— KYLE T. MOSLEY, *SPORTS ILLUSTRATED*

"One of the most talented sports anchors of our generation. He had his challenges in life, but he overcame them."

— JEFF HULLINGER, ATLANTA NEWS AND
SPORTS ANCHOR

"No matter what was thrown at him, he'd smile, handle it, and make us all better."

— SUZYN WALDMAN, YANKEES COLOR
COMMENTATOR

"Thank you for showing how it's done, Fred."

— WILLIE GEIST, *SUNDAY TODAY* HOST

For Mack, Gabrielle, and Sheila

CONTENTS

TV TIMELINE

1978–80 — WICS (Springfield, IL)
1980–84 — CNN/Turner Sports
1984–86 — WDIV-TV (Detroit, MI)
1986–01 — CNN/Turner Sports
1997–01 — *More Than a Game*/Raycom Sports
2002–04 — YES Network
2004–08 — ESPN
2008–11 — Fox Sports South
2011–15 — WVUE-DT (New Orleans, LA)
2015–18 — WVLA-TV (Baton Rouge, LA)
2018–19 — WDVM-TV (Hagerstown, MD)
2019–22 — Black News Channel

I first saw Fred Hickman the way millions of Americans did: on television. Growing up a Yankees fan in New York's Hudson Valley, I watched him on the YES Network and eventually ESPN. I had never imagined we would work together years later—certainly not at a local TV station in Baton Rouge, Louisiana—until it happened in 2017. We became newsroom colleagues, bagel-noshing brethren, mutual petsitters, and friends.

In early 2022, shortly after his liver cancer diagnosis, Fred asked me to help him write an autobiography. He saw a book as the perfect way to honor those who had uplifted him over the years. We zigzagged between chapters, topics, word-pictures, and plenty of laughs. To me, it was the privilege of a lifetime.

In what turned out to be his final weeks, Fred made his wishes explicit: We would write as many chapters as we could with whatever time was left. He still wanted his words published for the world to hold, read, and enjoy, even if he were no longer alive to sign a copy.

Fred died on November 9, 2022. After thought and reflection, members of the Hickman family encouraged me to keep his dream of publication alive. They volunteered background and insight that helped me finalize the existing manuscript. Their loving support is forever a gift.

This story may have required teamwork, but it will always be Fred's. The published anecdotes and dialogue were to the best of his memory. The opinions were his own. The voice was his.

And through all the changes to journalism, media, and the world at large since his death, his voice remains a compass.

Harrison Golden

CHANNELING

1

—————

STRAIGHT,
NO CHASER

MY FAVORITE DOCTORS, LIKE MY FAVORITE journalists, are the ones who tell it straight. Even if hearing the truth feels like getting slapped in the face with a wet towel.

"It's liver cancer, Fred."

At least I finally had an answer. For some time, I had wondered why I kept feeling drained, passing out, and waking up in hospitals unable to remember what year it was. I'd wondered why the injections doctors were giving me kept wearing off so quickly. Now I knew.

Maybe the diagnosis should have made me cry right away—or at least gotten me choked up or pale—but it didn't. Instead, I found myself looking past the doctor's desk. The reflection of the glass pane behind him reminded me of a studio camera lens. Beside me and holding my hand was Sheila, my wife and forever coanchor.

I rattled off more questions.

"What are my chances?"

"Will the treatment knock me out?"

"How can we beat it? How did previous patients beat it?"

He told me about two tumors. One looked isolated enough

that surgeons could at least get much of it. The other would hopefully go away through Y90 radioembolization, which involves going into my thigh and injecting radioactive glass microspheres. The idea, at least to a layman like me, was that the balls would make the cancer blow itself up. I would be out the whole time for each procedure.

"If that doesn't work," Doc said, "we'll have to get you on the transplant list."

"Is it anything like the NBA Draft?" I asked one of the nurses. It was my poor three-point shot at humor.

She laughed, which was nice of her. "You're a survivor from the moment you're diagnosed," she told me. "Don't forget that."

But just in case, I needed to get documents ready. Financial files. Passwords and account information. Last wills and testaments. Funeral instructions. Damn, all this is morbid.

The more I looked at all the death-related papers to leave behind, the more I admired how pages can breathe life. Inspiring me were personal writings from fighters I'm lucky to have known over the years. Not only had Turner Sports' Ernie Johnson and Craig Sager written touching books on their cancer battles, but ESPN's Robin Roberts and Stuart Scott had done the same. Mitch Albom, a valiant competitor from my Detroit sports stint, had authored *Tuesdays with Morrie*, about his late professor's grace through Lou Gehrig's disease. And I can't forget my daughter, Gabrielle, whose poetry gives me joy.

Yet when it came to chronicling my own life, I resisted. I doubted I could offer readers any new sage advice. Unlike other people's diagnoses, mine didn't shower me with wisdom. I didn't suddenly wish I had spent more time fishing. I didn't acquire any secrets to world peace. I left Doc's office feeling no more self-aware than when I had entered—and hardly as wise as the three Magi who had witnessed the birth of Jesus. What could I type that wasn't already available elsewhere?

Which brings me to another reason I didn't want to write this autobiography: One of the first things my parents taught me was to not have a rearview mirror. The past, after all, is the past. I hated the idea of looking back for even a minute let alone months or years. Besides, I had stared down enough blinking computer cursors in my day. However moving others' self-portraits were, I figured one by me would cause a crash.

Then again, I hadn't told my kids the diagnosis yet.

IF I KNOW anything about sports, it's that telling your son and daughter you have cancer isn't one. Practice doesn't make perfect, not this time. So instead of over-rehearsing words in front of a mirror until they meant nothing, I gave Mack and Gabby the raw truth they deserved about the news they didn't.

"I have cancer."

Once those words left my mouth, they hit me. I recalled how my kids had lost their mother at too young an age. I pictured them in church clothes as the grownups they now are. I imagined them someday in the future, crying without my shoulder. I couldn't help but cry myself, even if that someday wasn't today.

I owed it to them to show my full self. If that meant acquiring even a small rearview mirror—so I could leave them a more open account of my past—so be it. The people closest to me needed a chance to read how much they have mattered.

"I'm not down for the count yet," I told them. "I'll give this every fiber I've got."

We hugged and kissed. We whispered, as always, "I love you to the moon and back."

I looked out my window, spotted the moon, and took notes.

School picture day, circa 1965.

2

AIR FRED

My nine-year-old self couldn't fool anyone on Christmas morning 1965. I was wearing the toy I had just unwrapped as part of a neighborhood-wide secret Santa exchange. The toy was a Sixfinger, which was supposed to hook onto my index finger and blend in to resemble a sixth digit. It was a cool idea. But given the fake finger's Caucasian tones and my Blackness, the jig was up right away.

I asked my parents who would've gotten me this. "Whichever house it was," I told them, "I bet they knew it wouldn't look right on me!"

My father knelt down. "You don't know that," he told me as I sat on the floor. "I can't force you to play with it, but I do want you to talk about your neighbors with respect."

Both of my parents mentioned respect often because, in Springfield, Illinois, their families saw the ills that had come without it. In 1838, their ancestors witnessed a militia chase hundreds of indigenous people from Indiana through Springfield, part of what became known as the Potawatomi Trail of Death. In 1865, my great-great-grandfather mourned the assassination of a man whose hair he used to cut, a former Springfield lawyer named Abraham Lincoln. For three days in 1908, my grandparents hid as a mob of five thousand White people set Black-owned houses on fire, lynched men in the street, and destroyed Black-owned businesses. On October 17, 1956, I was named Fredrick Douglas Hickman after abolitionist Frederick Douglass, with a deliberate spelling that freed me to chart my own course. And with all the strife on *The Huntley-Brinkley Report* each night in the mid-1960s, Mom and Dad said I was lucky that my white house on Brown Street stood in a mostly peaceful integrated place.

Dad grabbed a brown marker and colored my Sixfinger to match my skin better. I tried to like his adjustment. Really. But now it just looked worse. The ink was drying in streaks. The shade was still too light. I told him thanks but no thanks.

He made it up to me days later. Still on my holiday break from school, I jumped at his offer to take me to work. He was the best janitor that Capital Airport had ever seen, and I could see what made him so passionate about the job. Once he finished his rounds, we spent an hour looking out the windows. We watched the tip of the air traffic control tower blink with the stars. We didn't say a word and didn't need to. The clear night said it all.

I fell in love with the air.

WHAT DREW me to radio was the feeling that the sky could talk. So I took my allowance savings to Radio Shack and ran home with a make-your-own-radio kit. It included a wire that I was supposed to attach to a pipe, essentially turning my house into an antenna. I didn't know the exact science, only that my bedroom window gave me the best reception. And unlike the Sixfinger, this toy didn't have a skin color.

For hours at a time, from under the covers, I'd hear the world. During baseball season, WGN would air Chicago Cubs games with announcers Vince Lloyd and Lou Boudreau. Sometimes I felt like spying on the rival St. Louis Cardinals, and Harry Caray and

Jack Buck would give me the scoop on KMOX. On cloudless nights, my humble setup caught glimmers of faraway powerhouses: WLW Cincinnati, WHO Des Moines, WSM Nashville, WWL New Orleans, even WBZ Boston and KOA Denver. Long before cable TV or the internet, the AM dial was my superhighway, complete with accents and street names I had never before heard.

I was twelve when I learned that broadcasting could pay the bills. As a member of Springfield's Junior Achievement chapter, I toured the inside of a local radio station for the first time. The action gripped me. A board operator pressed buttons like they were keys on a piano. An announcer stormed down the hall waving copy. The needles inside the VU meters swayed. Clocks ticked everywhere. I wanted more.

Finally, the moment of truth. The tour's last stop was the live studio. The host gave everyone in my group a chance to say their names into the microphone. About a half-dozen kids took their turns, then I took mine.

"I'm Fred Hickman."

Of course. Leave it to me to experience puberty during my first on-air appearance. I sounded nothing like myself. This voice was weird. Deeper.

The station's program director flung open the studio door. "Who was that?" he asked.

All the other kids pointed at me. Usually they only did that whenever I broke a window playing stickball. I figured I was in trouble again for some reason.

The program director placed his hand on my shoulder.

"Wanna play records?"

BETWEEN PART-TIME WORK at the radio station and budding athletic stardom, teenage "Air Fred" was taking flight. I had the nickname *before* someone named Michael became "Air Jordan." (Yeah, I nicknamed myself. Sue me.)

I began freshman year at Springfield Southeast High determined to play basketball, but there was a catch. Because every underclassman wanted to join the junior varsity hoops squad—and almost no one wanted to play for the lousy football team—the school made football a prerequisite for basketball. The move was meant to filter out the candidate pool and boost Southeast's gridiron cred. I didn't like it, but if wearing a hopefully good helmet got me closer to Spartans basketball, rules were rules.

On the late afternoon of my football tryout, the coach shouted at me right away. "Hickman! On your back!"

I had to do what's called a hamburger drill. Just hearing the coach say "hamburger drill," especially at 4:30 p.m., made me hungry.

"Hey, this is no time to eat!" he yelled. "The tackler will have a ten-yard run at you! When you hear my whistle, you'd better turn over, get on your feet, and stop him!"

"Yes, sir," I replied. "Who's my tackler?"

The coach didn't say an answer. He only snapped his fingers to summon my executioner.

From the sidelines strutted Herb McMath. If that name sounds familiar, it's because he later played defensive tackle for the 1976 Super Bowl Champion Oakland Raiders. At this point, he was a senior on Southeast's varsity team. Lucky me.

Coach gave his order. "McMath! Go!"

From my view on the twenty-yard line, as I maintained a casket-ready position, the six-foot-four-inch beast charging at me seemed twelve feet fall. That's all I remember.

Next thing I knew, my helmet was cracked. I struggled to catch my breath. In my mouth were dirt and grass, which tasted nothing like a hamburger. Had I eaten before that tackle, we would've had an even bigger mess on the field.

I quit football then and there. This was way above my pay

grade—which, for this high school freshman, was zero. I had no problem cheering in the stands, even making funny faces into the local TV sports reporter's camera, but playing this sport just wasn't for me.

A year later came my next chance at hardwood fame. This time, aspiring basketball players who didn't want to play football could run cross-country instead, so I tried out for that. But a half-mile into the required two-mile run around Bunn Park, I started feeling winded. I spotted a cab driver and got him to drive me toward the finish line. I bolted out of the Lincoln Town Car and finished midway through the pack, far ahead enough to impress yet far behind enough to thwart suspicion. Nailed it.

I was in. My name finally made the basketball roster. My jersey and shorts fit just right. Ladies winked. Life was good.

Just sitting on the Spartans' bench was enough for me to daydream about my future. I imagined myself landing a full ride to the University of Illinois and sporting the Fighting Illini blue and orange. I could sign a sneaker contract. I could win a Most Valuable Player Award as a Chicago Bull.

The problem, however, was that I barely left the bench. I spent most games seated and sticking my tongue at nearby cameras. A few months into my sophomore year, my uniform remained the only one in Southeast High history that had never needed washing. I saw no need to clean something I hadn't sweated in.

That all changed one night in 1972. We were playing against a school from Decatur. Doubting I would play this game either, I wore silk underwear.

"Hickman," the coach said. "Get out there."

I looked at him and thought he was joking.

"Get out there! Go!"

He was serious.

And so was I. I sprinted onto the court so quickly, I forgot to remove the sideline towel from my shoulders.

My only goal in mind was scoring. It was the only way a junior-varsity boy could get his name in the newspaper. Assists, rebounds, and fouls didn't matter. What mattered was putting the ball into the basket.

My friend Leo got the jump ball. I let out a blood-curdling plea for a pass and got my wish. At last, my beloved.

My path was clear. Nothing stood between me and two points. I dribbled toward the basket and heard folks yelling, "No! No!"; I assumed they were Decatur fans and kept going. Then came the most gorgeous lay-up I had ever seen. My fingers rolled on cue. The ball arced into the net. I celebrated with an airplane pose. I was back, baby.

But nobody cheered my name. No one clapped or waved signs for the hometown Spartans. No love. Only dead silence. Had I gone deaf?

The first audible reaction was a hyena-like laugh ten seconds later from Bill, the class clown. I had apparently outdone him. I had scored on the wrong side of the floor.

I learned some lessons. One was that I shouldn't get ahead of myself. And though my mishap still got me a mention in the local paper, I also realized I probably wouldn't go pro.

If Air Fred ever wanted to walk onto a professional playing surface again, it would have to be on air. I would have to be a sportscaster.

IF YOU'VE HEARD of Coe College in Cedar Rapids, Iowa, I'm impressed. Not many people have. I only learned about it because my high school transcript had somehow gotten into their hands, leading the school's admissions office to offer me a free ride. At this point, my dream school was Pepperdine University in Malibu, California, but let's be real: Had I gotten into Pepperdine, I would've spent all my time at the beach without ever graduating. So Coe College it was.

What the school lacked in a formal communications or journalism program I gained in hands-on experience. While other dudes lived it up in their frat houses late at night, I would sleep in the office of campus radio station KCOE-FM, saying goodnight to the control board, microphone, and record library. One morning, as the frat bros woke up hungover, the station's outgoing music director named me his successor.

And I had a paid gig on the side. It was at a rock-and-roll station, KLWW, 1450 on the AM dial. I played records and read some on-air promotions, including one for Hawaiian Tropic oil. As a thank-you for reading the promo copy a few more times, someone at Hawaiian Tropic sent me a few dozen bottles of tanning oil, more than any man with melanin would ever need in his life. I didn't need a suntan, because I had been born with one! So I went around Coe's campus, sold the oil bottles, and made some extra bucks. Not too shabby.

This pocket of Iowa was also where this young disc jockey saw, proverbially speaking, the other side of the record. Not once as a kid in Springfield had anyone called me the "n" word—you know, the racial slur that ends with a hard "r"—but while I was driving off campus one day, a pack of guys in a nearby car shouted it right at me and sped off. All I had done was drive the speed limit, look straight ahead, stay in my lane, and have dark skin. I hadn't done anything to provoke them, not that that should ever matter anyway.

I wondered behind the wheel. Who else had they shouted that word at? What other words had they used about other people? Who else might have called me that one particular word behind my back over the years?

Once I returned to campus, I reminded myself that the guys who had spewed that word didn't know me personally. Judging by their language, they didn't care to know much about anything. The reason they had driven away so quickly was because they were too cowardly to face the consequences of their words. They were too chicken to show compassion. They were only cheating themselves.

Still, I'd be lying if I said I wasn't upset. It's like what my high school health teacher once said, albeit referencing an entirely different life event: "You never forget your first time."

There weren't many Black students at Coe, but the few who were there helped me reflect on the highway experience. For eight consecutive nights in January 1977, about a dozen of us huddled around a big TV inside the student union to watch the miniseries *Roots* on ABC. To be with people who looked like me, to see episodes that featured characters who looked like us, and to see those characters endure capture, slave ships, hard labor, whippings, and post-slavery violence opened my eyes. That we were here, watching this show together on a college campus, was a testament to the generations before us. We were the fruits of our ancestors' willpower.

Seeing how TV had brought my small college group together, I wanted in, but it wasn't easy. After graduating, I applied to jobs at TV stations across the country and heard nothing back. Months passed without responses. You might understandably think this was because I lacked TV experience, but one manager in Waterloo had his own reason. Only after I drove to that station's studio, located about an hour northwest of Coe's campus, and knocked on the front door did the boss admit the truth: "I'm sorry. This town is not ready to see a person of color on television."

Thankfully, one TV market was ready: home. After a few months of spinning country tunes at WFMB-FM in Springfield, I heard from a former Southeast High classmate's cousin, a woman named Lynne White. She was moving to St. Louis and leaving her reporting job at WICS Channel 20, the same station that had tolerated my goofy high school sports photobombs. She told me the news director, who also anchored, wanted someone who could cover sports. That the boss's name was Don Hickman—no relation—offered a good laugh before we got down to business.

. . .

CHANNEL 20 WAS a great place to learn and make mistakes. Like today's multimedia journalists, I was a one-man band who shot, wrote, tracked, and edited video, except the gear back then weighed way more. The camera could whack someone in the face if I wasn't careful. The film reels I used seemed a thousand times bigger than today's memory cards, and they stored nowhere near as much footage.

Don was a more patient boss than I probably deserved, as proven when I substituted for station weatherman Flip Spiceland. To compensate for my meteorological ineptitude, I decided that the best way to show storm conditions would be to open the garage door that shielded the news set from nature's elements. For a few seconds, the studio camera captured the rain and winds so crisply . . . until those same winds knocked that camera off its axis, out the door, and down the hilly driveway. The camera operator, who had failed to lock the equipment in place, couldn't chase it fast enough. Broken glass everywhere.

The more I messed up, the more I respected Don. His calm tone carried the newsroom. He forgave mistakes not only because he knew what doing each job was like, but also because he was simply that kind of guy. He could have entered any other industry and become just as big a mentor.

Even so, Springfield didn't feel much like home anymore. Dad's death some time earlier, following years with diabetes, had left marks all over my childhood house. His toolbox collected dust. The bar he had built in our basement, featuring glass bricks and multicolored lights, looked duller. The clotheslines where Mom would hang the freshest-smelling laundry still waved in the summer breeze but with fewer button-downs and slacks. I could still hear the accordion teacher next door playing "Lady of Spain," but his arms didn't squeeze so fast anymore.

The city's deeper changes bled into my work. With a short staff and no major-league teams within a hundred-or-so-mile radius, I had little choice but to cover fewer games and more crimes. I filmed a once-promising classmate's perp walk outside the Sangamon County Jail. I reported on a murder blocks from where my mother and siblings still lived. Police tape lined what had been makeshift stickball fields.

My journalistic adage—"Don't Become the Story"—became tougher to follow in my birth city. After I got to the scene of a standoff, a hostage-taker recognized me from his window. It turned out we knew one another from way back when. So an officer handed me a bullhorn and told me to tell him to surrender. I complied because I didn't want to piss off a cop with a gun. "Listen, I'm not telling you what to do," I told the captor, "but if I were you, I'd come out and let the woman go." The guy gave up within minutes. I went home questioning how objective a reporter I could be in my hometown. Maybe it was time to move.

Flip told me about Atlanta. He was moving there to do weather at a soon-to-be-launched 24/7 channel called the Cable News Network. Though most news outlets at the time had relegated sports to the last two minutes of a newscast, he told me this place would devote a whole nightly show to the day's scores and stories. He said there were still plenty of job openings.

I had a few reasons not to apply. Not only did this channel not have its headquarters in New York, home of most national media outlets; it was in Atlanta, of all cities. Viewers would only be able to watch on cable television. I knew almost nobody with cable. Plus I had just gotten an offer to anchor weekend news in Dayton for just as much money—at a TV station that seemed less likely than CNN to go belly-up within the year.

Conflicted, I went where I did my best thinking: a baseball stadium. I had a box seat for the minor-league Springfield Redbirds at Lanphier Park.

As it turned out, two baseball legends had tickets as well.

Near me sat Satchel Paige and Cool Papa Bell. Both were in

their seventies by this point, and Satchel needed an oxygen tank to breathe, but their love for the game remained timeless. After I said hello, they invited me to sit with them. They wanted to talk baseball. The three of us.

I still pinch myself over the hour-long conversation that followed. Satchel and Cool Papa told me about their years in the Negro Leagues, spent shuttling to and from "coloreds-only" hotels across the South. Satchel recalled the time he'd told batter Josh Gibson which pitches he was going to throw and where—and still struck Gibson out. That long-ago at-bat still made him laugh, oxygen and all. Baseball had been good to them, even when much of the country wasn't. My only regret from that day is that because I was off work, I had no camera to record their brilliance.

But the memory lived on in a different way. It set the example for the kind of journalist I yearned to be. I wanted to show what sports can teach us about ourselves. I wanted to tell stories of people who had bettered the world through games. I wanted to meet rising stars, reintroduce forgotten talents, and give underappreciated names their due credit. Maybe I'd even make new friends.

I sent CNN my demo reel and buckled up.

Graduating from Coe College, 1978.

Interviewing Joe Shaheen, owner of the since-closed Springfield Speedway, for WICS in Springfield, Illinois.

3

'A NEW BALLGAME'

I didn't ask why the state trooper had pulled me over. I just gave him what he asked for.

"License and registration."

"Yes, sir."

He looked at the license then back at me. I couldn't see his eyes, only his bubbled neck shifting down and back up.

"So you're a Yankee."

"Well, actually a Cubs fan."

His neck stayed put for a few seconds. He flicked my license back at me. I guess he assumed I was being snarky, but I honestly thought the term applied only to Northeasterners. I was just some guy from Illinois.

"Here, you're a Yankee," he said. "I'm letting you go. But stay outta trouble . . . and welcome to Georgia."

I had gotten the CNN job in Atlanta. On the Saturday before my first day, I decided to explore what was then the most visited tourist site in all of Georgia: Stone Mountain. Some folks near my new apartment had told me the place offered panoramic views of the Atlanta skyline. So I paid to park, took in the blue skies and granite-lined landscape, and whiffed the spring air while strolling to the ticket booth.

The woman at the booth leaned forward and cricked her neck.

"Um, are you sure you want to be here?" she asked me.

"Of course! It's a gorgeous day."

"Okay, but I'm glad to give your money back if you change your mind."

I pooh-poohed her disclaimer as something she probably told everyone. I took my ticket and set off to admire the mountain views. Ahh, nature!

Walking a few dozen feet more, something wasn't right. I saw white robes circling in the distance. Then pointy white hoods.

It hit me. These were Ku Klux Klan members. I was walking into a Klan rally.

Anyone who says Michael Jackson came up with the moonwalk is dead wrong. I invented it in May 1980 while fleeing Stone Mountain.

I got my money back and sped off before the robed men could see me.

MY FIRST DAY at CNN marked another culture shock. The channel's headquarters didn't fill some tall urban office building. It was in a ninety-thousand-square-foot mansion on the grounds of a former country club. White columns and a circular driveway graced the front. Swimming pools had occupied the back. Too bad I had left my Speedo at home.

Scratch that. Maybe a hazmat suit would've been better.

It turned out the newsroom was in the basement. Construction crews were rushing to fix the damage caused by its previous non-paying occupants: Georgia Tech frat bros and rats. Sawing, buzzing, and hammering caused walls to vibrate. Water and other fluids dripped from the ceiling, sometimes into buckets and other times onto the mud where floors hadn't been installed yet. And with only one working toilet in the entire building, the most important rule was "DON'T LOSE THE BATHROOM KEY."

I waded through the obstacle course and found my desk. Covering it was a thick binder of an onboarding manual. One page said something like this: "The three networks have owned the airwaves for too long. Now CNN is starting a new ballgame."

A new ballgame? Much of the world was doubting CNN would even take the field! Newspaper critics argued that founder Ted Turner lacked any experience or interest in news; the only newscast on his SuperStation TBS aired at three in the morning, with a German shepherd for a coanchor. Inside the newsroom, at least one workplace comrade likened our logo to two snakes who were . . . shall we say *mating*? Our predictions on how many months the experiment would last lowered with each botched rehearsal.

Yet something stopped me from quitting. Not money. Certainly not job security. It was the idea that the whole network could metaphorically and physically collapse at any time. It encouraged me even more to give each day my all. Such uncertainty probably would have frustrated me had I been older or joined CNN from ABC, NBC, or CBS, but as a twenty-three-year-old new to the national scene, I embraced the rush.

Having bosses with meaningful visions also helped. News executive Reese Schonfeld's open-floor newsroom placed the sports department within the same four walls as general assignment, weather, business, and politics, which helped when big stories demanded perspective from more than one beat. Sports boss Bill MacPhail—the former CBS Sports president who had once told Pat Summerall, "I'll never get mad at you for saying too little"—instilled firm but calm storytelling. And by hoisting a United Nations flag above CNN's headquarters, Ted told everyone that this channel's reporting would better the world.

The global interest reached the front of my desk. On the afternoon of June 1, 1980, a pack of strangers mumbling a language other than English followed a Southern-drawl-speaking tour guide. I normally would've picked up my head and waved hello, but with just hours until our launch, I had no time and no correction tape. I wrote like hell on my Smith-Corona typewriter, trying not to make a mistake that would force me to rip out a paper and start over again. Then one of the visitors' cameras produced a blinding flash.

"Here's where we're gonna do sports," the guy with the drawl told the visitors. "Hey, Fred!"

I should've been nicer to him, but my nerves and temporary blindness were leaving me on edge.

"Do you mind?" I blurted out.

The guy started laughing. "Ahh, you're busy! I get it."

Only after he and his group walked away did I regain the sight to realize. The guy I had just told to buzz off was Ted Turner. *Oops.*

A short time later, I found him and apologized.

"No need," he said, cigar in hand. "Hell, I got a kick out of it. Just the attitude this place needs!"

His reaction told me all I needed to know. Sure, his nicknames included "Captain Outrageous" and "The Mouth of the South," but he could also turn an awkward situation into a confidence booster.

I returned to my desk to finish hammering out scripts for that night. But first, I noticed the time: 5:59.

CNN PREMIERED AT SIX P.M. Eastern time with video of a mission statement. From outside the headquarters, Ted recited from a sheet of paper: "To provide information to people when it wasn't available before; to offer those who want it a choice; for the American people, whose thirst for understanding and a better life has made this venture possible; for the cable industry, whose pioneering spirit caused this great step forward in communication; and for those employees of Turner Broadcasting, whose total commitment to their company has brought us here today, I dedicate the news channel for America . . . the Cable News Network."

A military band played the National Anthem. A camera zoomed in on the garden of satellite dishes behind the building. A narrator rattled off a list of cities foreign and domestic, each one overlapping the last. The control room gave the anchors their cue.

"Good evening, I'm David Walker."

"And I'm Lois Hart. Now here's the news."

Lois's four improvised words said it all. No gimmicks. No telling viewers how to think. No masquerading opinions as news. Just the news.

Or in my case, just the sports.

We had plenty to cover. New York Yankees star Reggie Jackson had gotten a .38-caliber revolver pulled on him over a Manhattan parking space. John Mahaffey had won golf's Kemper Open by five under par. For the second time in as many weeks, someone had broken the world pole vault record. Horse racing's Belmont Stakes were less than a week away. And in an exclusive interview with my colleagues Bob Kurtz and Nick Charles, NFL Commissioner Pete Rozelle said the Oakland Raiders' plan to defy the league and move to Los Angeles would incur a legal marathon. As far as sportscasts went, Bob and Nick offered a half-hour masterclass at seven o'clock.

My job that night was to man the shorter segments. The first one, with coanchor Dan Carney, aired at 7:30 and was essentially a ten-minute "In Case You Missed May" crash course. We recapped the New York Islanders' Stanley Cup victory, Johnny Rutherford's Indy 500 win, and baseball's eleventh-hour aversion of a strike. Then over a synth-disco version of "Take Me Out to the Ball Game," we aired a montage of major-league bloopers, including one of the Toronto Blue Jays mascot twerking before that was even a thing.

I got caught in a blooper myself. During the eight o'clock newscast with Lou Waters and Reynelda Muse, I ended a sports cut-in by saying, "Now back to Reynelda at the anchor desk." But instead of the monitor showing Reynelda (a Black woman), it stayed on Lou (a White man). Lou paused and smiled. "I'm definitely not Reynelda at the anchor desk," he told viewers. In the spirit of live TV, we took it all in stride.

I was just glad we had survived the evening.

MANY COWORKERS and I still doubted CNN would last. Prognosticators claimed the network would hemorrhage millions in its opening months and, with luck, break even after a few years. Even those who believed in our mission predicted that a larger competitor would soon dwarf us into oblivion.

But one sports anchor clung to hope.

"We'll be alright," Nick Charles told me. "Slim Whitman will save us."

A nearby TV was set to TBS, which at that point was almost singlehandedly funding CNN. A commercial was on. It was for country yodeler Slim Whitman's greatest hits album: *All My Best*, twenty classic songs for $7.98.

The two of us devised a theory: As long as viewers kept buying that album—which they did—we would stay on the air. "Pretty soon," Nick said with a smile, "we'll all be singing 'Una Paloma Blanca!'"

In retrospect, Nick's charm shouldn't have surprised me. Born Nicholas Charles Nickeas to a Greek family, he had paid his way through college by driving cabs in Chicago, a job that demands both urgency and people skills. He had always gotten passengers where they needed to go; this job would be no different.

He seemed so much larger than life on air, I almost forgot we had worked at the same small newsroom in Springfield, albeit at different times. He had covered sports at WICS Channel 20 a few years before me, back when he was twenty-four and I was a four-teen-year-old high school freshman.

Leave it to him to remember.

"Quick question," he said. "When I covered Southeast High games for Channel 20, there was this one kid who never stopped waving at my camera and shouting, 'Put me on TV! Put me on TV!' Was that you?"

I raised my hands. "Guilty as charged."

As great as his memory was, we were about to make even better ones.

Collectively representing, at the time of this photo with Nick, more than 100 years of consecutive championship-less seasons.

Drawn and sent by a loyal CNN viewer.

4

THE HICK AND NICK SHOW

I don't know if management simply liked how my Afro complemented Nick's Spartan mane, but whatever the reason, Nick and I became coanchors of CNN's nightly sports show.

"What should we call it?" a producer asked me in the hallway one day.

"It's a sports show, right?" I asked in return.

"Yeah."

"Nightly?"

"Yeah."

"What about *Sports Tonight*?"

"Voila!"

It was that simple.

Simplicity, after all, was the point. Unlike *SportsCenter*, which had launched nine months earlier on a new sports-only channel called ESPN, CNN's *Sports Tonight* was but one spoke in a diverse news wheel. With Lou Dobbs's *Moneyline* as our lead-in, we didn't exactly wield a built-in audience of jocks. We had to win crowds on our own and make a sports show that anyone could appreciate. We had to tell viewers about sports stuff—the simple and the complex—without acting stuffy or seeming like meat-heads. News chief Reese Schonfeld said it best when he told us he wanted a program that "every bar in the country will have on."

Nick's writing fit the goal. Whenever he found a working type-writer, he would run for a Sharpie and inscribe "NICK" along the side, and that's when the real magic would start. Maybe it was his love for the art of conversation. Maybe it was whatever he kept spraying onto his scalp. Either way, he could break down informa-tion in a way that transported viewers. If you couldn't attend Larry Holmes's defeat of Muhammad Ali or Roberto Durán's "no más" surrender to Sugar Ray Leonard, Nick could take you closer than anyone. He could write about a racehorse and make you think it was a person.

People think I'm lying when I say Nick and I never argued, but it's true. At least once a night, he or I would think up either a top story, a highlight to use, or a postgame soundbyte to clip—and the other would blurt out the same suggestion. He sought my exper-tise on basketball, and I his on boxing. The fun we had went beyond an overused term like *chemistry*. It more closely resembled jazz. We played off one another's strengths.

Fine, we disagreed on one thing. He liked the Chicago White Sox, which I clearly did not. But even that deepened our brother-hood. By 1980, his Sox had gone sixty-three years without a World Series title, and my Cubs had gone seventy-two. From April's hopelessly wide eyes to October's thumb-twiddling, we both knew the underdog fan's life.

In a way, our fandoms had taught us to keep cheering through the punches. During the 1981 baseball strike, viewers called to complain. They didn't want us to cover free agency or player arbi-tration, even though disagreements over these issues were what had caused the stoppage in the first place. "Just stick to reading scores," one caller told me. "This is sports, not Econ 101."

Other people didn't know we existed at all. Detroit Tigers manager Sparky Anderson was among them.

"Mr. Anderson, this is Nick Charles with CNN," Nick said one day while standing over his desk phone. "We'd love to have you as a guest on our—"

Anderson interrupted mid-sentence. "I don't need a fucking loan!" Then he hung up.

Nick paused for a few seconds before placing down his phone.

"You alright?" I asked him.

"I think Sparky just confused CNN with Citizens National Bank."

We had some publicizing to do.

"YOU KNOW what the public would love, Fred? You announcing games," Ted Turner said late one night in October 1981. "You ever do color commentary?"

I wondered if Ted was just sleepwalking. After all, he had a habit of roaming the building—often unshaven, barefoot, and in a robe—during hours normally reserved for either *Sports Tonight* staffers or insomniacs. Nonetheless, I went with it.

"Sure," I said. "A few times."

That was a lie. I had never called a live sporting event, not even a play. But at age twenty-four, in front of a boss who would become America's largest private landowner, I didn't know the meaning of "no."

"Then you're my guy!" Ted told me.

He unpacked the details. Within days, I would travel with the NBA's Atlanta Hawks. Our destination would be the Texas Tech campus in Lubbock. There the Hawks, whom Ted owned, would play the San Antonio Spurs in a preseason game to air on TBS, which Ted also owned. Set to join play-by-play guy Skip Caray was yours truly, who would turn twenty-five that night. I couldn't imagine a cooler birthday gift.

I rode the plane then swaggered onto the team's charter bus.

"Where do the announcers usually sit?" I asked the players.

"Usually behind the driver," one said.

Skip was in Dallas and planned to meet us in Lubbock later that afternoon, so I took the player's word for it. I snapped my fingers, shuffled to the front, and sat. Legroom galore.

Then I detected a six-foot-three-inch shadow.

"Hey, what are you doing?" the shadow said.

It was Kevin Loughery, the Hawks' head coach.

"Coach, I'm doing color for the game," I told him.

"That's wonderful. But you're sitting in my seat."

All the Hawks players busted out laughing. I suddenly realized they had told me to sit up front as a practical joke. They were all in on it. A few of them patted my back afterwards to thank me for being a good sport. I guess the rookie announcer had it coming.

The next plot twist was no prank. A thunderstorm was stranding Skip in Dallas. The producer tasked with stat-keeping was also stuck. With game time nearing, they were both still more than three hundred miles from the arena. They wouldn't make it. Not only would I not have anyone to bounce color commentary off of, but I would have to do play-by-play—which I had never done before—and do it solo on a nationally broadcast superstation. I was sweating through my tie.

The TBS crew wound up finding a college student to keep stats. But nice as he was, he had never seen a basketball game in his life.

The Hawks got into early foul trouble. I turned to the college kid. "They've got *how* many fouls already?"

He shrugged.

He confessed during a timeout. "I know nothing of basketball. I'm a soccer guy."

I needed a drink.

After the game's long-awaited end, I changed clothes and hit up a country-and-western bar. The joint evoked *Bonanza*, cowboy hats and all. Dudes walked in, spat tobacco onto the floor, and walked through their saliva puddles wearing head-to-toe rawhide.

And here I was with a tracksuit, sneakers, and ballcap.

My fellow patrons were none too pleased with my fashion choices. At the payphone, as I waited to call my mother, a few sneers and stares came my way. One saloon cowboy looked like he wanted to off me. By the time my turn at the phone came and Mom wished me a happy birthday, I warned her, "Mom, I may be coming home soon." I didn't tell her that my homecoming would probably involve a bodybag.

Yet I somehow lived to see the next morning. After breakfast, hoping to fit in and avoid fisticuffs during any future West Texas visits, I embarked on a cowboy's shopping spree. Leather boots? Check. Oversized hat? Check. Circular belt buckle with a gun shape in the middle? Check. I boarded the Hawks' flight back to Georgia later that day lugging everything but a horse.

I returned to my Atlanta flat that evening feeling like I'd been in a gunfight. I threw off the boots and struggled to distinguish toes from blisters. I loosened the belt buckle, which had pressed against my bladder for hours. Conceding that sweatpants would be comfier, I unzipped. My wedgie-inducing jeans, with the buckle still attached, hit the floor.

All of a sudden, the gun-shaped piece of the buckle snapped off and slid across the room. I walked over to see if I could reattach it. The closer I got, the more it resembled a real firearm.

Yep, it was a real firearm—trigger and all. I hadn't known it at the time of purchase, but apparently belt buckles with attached derringers are a thing. Nobody had told me. Nobody on the Hawks charter bus to the airport had seemed to notice. No security agents had stopped me from open-carrying an unlicensed gun onto a commercial plane. (This was obviously before 9/11.)

I realized then, in the middle of my apartment, in my boxer shorts, that I really had become a cowboy.

· · ·

THOUGH I DIDN'T BRING the derringer to work, I did return to the newsroom with a secret weapon: a plan to incorporate play-by-play into *Sports Tonight*. Sure, league restrictions barred us from showing sporting events live, but what could stop us from watching games on monitors and telling viewers what we were seeing? Fellow Illinoisan Ronald Reagan, who at this point was president of the United States, had basically done the same decades earlier, using telegraphs of Cubs games to recreate the plays for an Iowa radio station. If it helped "The Gipper," maybe it would give Hick and Nick an edge.

We finally tried my idea in the heat of summer. Baseball was the only major team sport around in those months, so we needed to stretch for time somehow. I looked down at a black-and-white TV that faced the anchor desk. A West Coast game was still on. "Alright, here's Ozzie Smith at the dish," I said in my best Jack Buck voice. "Cards have men on second and third. Now the pitch."

The doggone scheme worked too well. A few weeks into it, a higher-up from Major League Baseball called and said we were infringing on other channels' broadcast rights. We had to stop or else. Word of the league's warning got to Ted, who proceeded to tell me, "Yeah, I guess we should probably stop. But what the hell, at least you tried. The fact that the league yelled means people are watchin'!"

Our live look-in bit ended too soon, but its legacy endures. Decades later, ESPN and MLB Network would begin cutting into regular programming to relay live local feeds of great games in progress, albeit with league permission. And to any big-league announcer tired of reciting what has since become a mandatory in-game disclaimer—*"Any accounts or descriptions of this game may not be disseminated without the express written consent of Major League Baseball"*—I take the blame. Live and learn.

· · ·

THE GOOD NEWS was that Ted, Reese Schonfeld, Bill MacPhail, and others still encouraged me and Nick to keep thinking big. We sometimes flopped, like when I went on air dressed as a swami with a crystal ball. But without breathing Nielsen ratings down our necks, the bosses always trusted us to recover. Trial and error guided each night.

With an end-of-show segment called "Play of the Day," we struck gold at last. It started as a way to highlight the night's most eye-popping sports moment—often a walk-off homer or half-court shot—but it grew to include more. Long before TikTok or even *America's Funniest Home Videos*, everyday people began sending us their own videos of athletic feats and flubs. With more tapes came more viewers, many watching to see if their submission would appear.

My favorite PODs, as we nicknamed them, celebrated the wacky. A jet-skiing squirrel. A toilet-bowl-throwing contest. A rubber duck race down the Arkansas River. A quest to see which romantic could kiss a car the longest. A mailman outside Wrigley Field snagging a home run ball and skipping into the sunset. And dare we forget when a high school basketball player dashed off the court, dribbled down the hall, then reentered the gymnasium through another door and made his basket. We showed them all in the years that followed.

In the process, audiences shaped *Sports Tonight* into appointment television. Praise showered me and Nick from all directions. At Fulton County Stadium, where Ted would give CNN employees Braves tickets like candy, spectators would ignore the game and approach me instead. Some told me they liked how we would cover one sport at a time, as opposed to *SportsCenter*'s usual assortment. Even viewers who hadn't followed sports would say we were hip and smooth enough to spark their interest. Ratings books put us atop ESPN. And despite my *Welcome Back, Kotter*-esque poof, a scribe or two fancied our style. "Doesn't have the same ring as Huntley and Brinkley," one *Boston Globe* columnist wrote years later, "but Chet and David never had hair like Fred and Nick."

The rest of our channel was growing as well. The year 1982 brought CNN2, a spinoff that eventually became CNN Headline News. In 1983, CNN scored a victory when the rival Satellite News Channel went bye-bye after just over a year. By 1984, the Cable News Network was in twenty-six million homes, up from two million in 1980. And sure enough, Ted's all-news venture became poised to turn a profit by 1985.

But Nick and I were still just two Illinois kids who, like our viewers, enjoyed unwinding after the day. Many nights, we'd finish work at 2:30 a.m. and head to this one bar on Peachtree Street. The place would close to the general public at two o'clock, but the head keeper—a former Georgia Bulldogs football player—kept the taps flowing just for us.

Sometimes I wouldn't leave the bar until just before sunrise. Atlanta had less of a major-city feel then, so traffic didn't feel as gruesome. At times on my way home, streets would be downright silent.

The quiet led my mind to drift. I started thinking of the cities we had jetted to since CNN's launch. Despite gratitude, I couldn't help but sense a wall between myself and the athletes whom I had traveled hundreds or thousands of miles to interview. Did they think I was just another coast-to-coast parachuter? Someone only hungry for the soundbite? Someone who'd ring out a subject's emotions then bolt like a one-night stand? Because I had seen other national media outlets mistreat players as such, I understood why an athlete might feel uneasy around me.

I began to envy the local sports embeds. Even if they didn't meet as many figures as the national guys, they seemed to cover their respective cities' teams with far more depth. They could chat with the same folks every week, or even every day, and form more organic bonds. I had gotten a touch of that intimacy in Atlanta, through my select Hawks games and sports briefs for TBS, but not nearly to the extent I wanted. Besides, in those early days of CNN, larger-market local stations were still offering higher pay than Turner Broadcasting was.

So I returned to the Midwest, this time in a bigger city than Springfield. I got married and got a job in Detroit, home of teams in all four major American sports leagues. I could get to know Lions, Tigers, Red Wings, and Pistons—*oh, my!* On days off, my new wife and I could visit some Great Lakes.

Just one problem. I had forgotten my paddle.

5

———

BAD CHEMISTRY

The City of Detroit held a fireworks parade upon my arrival. Not long after that, thousands of people ran, held big signs, and cheered in the streets. Still house-hunting at the time, I was living in a downtown hotel room—a bird's eye view of all the excitement.

All for *me*?

Not quite. It was Summer 1984. The fireworks were for the Fourth of July. The running and big signs were for the Emily Detroit Run, the Motor City's annual ten-kilometer foot race.

But it did feel like, everywhere I went that year, celebrations followed. I became WDIV-TV's weekday sports reporter and weekend anchor in July, on the heels of Jack Morris's April no-hitter and the Tigers' 35-5 start to baseball's regular season. On the night the team beat Milwaukee to clinch the American League East title, six-foot-four-inch hurler Dave "The Rose" Rozema interrupted my locker room interview with legend Al Kaline in epic fashion—*BOOM!*—with a shaving cream pie right to my face. Not as tasty as whipped cream, but I took it as a sign; I was on their good side. Plus the 104-58 record and World Series glory that October were pretty darn sweet on their own.

34

One more thing. Sparky Anderson, the same Tigers manager who had confused CNN for a bank some years earlier, finally knew my name.

The natural highs of 1984 were hard acts to follow.

Even tougher to beat, as I learned over the next two winters, were the narcotic highs.

I DON'T LIKE to make excuses, so I won't. What I will say is that shortly after I found a Detroit address of my own, I accepted my new neighbor's offer of freebase cocaine. I tried it once. Then I bought some for myself and used again. And again. You get the idea.

In trying to justify my addiction, I became a mental gymnast. I told myself cocaine was giving me the energy to be the sports world's master truth-teller, even as hiding my use became its own job. I told myself the drug was making me good enough for a pay raise, yet it made me $400-a-week poorer. I told myself it would make me less lonely, though it ended my young marriage and brought paranoia. Whenever anyone smiled or said they recognized me, I suspected they were just milking me for free game tickets.

A third-round knockout dealt me a reality check. I was in the second row at Caesars Palace in Las Vegas, covering Detroit boxer Tommy Hearns's April 1985 fight against Marvin Hagler. Hearns appeared close to death, staggering in the ring, unable to stay up. His eyes rolled back. His handlers carried his limp body back into his corner.

The defeat had nothing to do with drugs—and everything to do with Hagler's brute force—but for a moment I saw myself in Hearns. The question wasn't whether cocaine would kill me. The question was who, if anyone, would carry my body when death came.

Still, I kept using in all sorts of ways. I returned to Detroit the next day and reloaded. Tired of forging elaborate reasons for taking hits, I decided I could use pipes and straws without having to explain myself. I could give anyone who asked a simple answer: "Not your business."

Except it was Bob Warfield's business. He was my boss at WDIV. The day I called out sick for the umpteenth time, citing my third "twenty-four-hour bug" in a month, he said his piece over the phone. "You sure that's all it is? You've been sick a lot lately."

"It'll pass," I replied. "See you tomorrow."

I hung up. Maybe I wouldn't see him tomorrow. Maybe I'd trek a few dozen miles to Ontario, a few thousand more to the Yukon, and never return. Either way, feeling guilty in my apartment all day wouldn't have helped. So I got in my Thunderbird coupe and drove.

I cruised down Five Mile Road before stopping at a convenience store. I bought a newspaper.

The sports section saved my life. It included a story on athletes who had almost died from drugs. In the store's parking lot, I sat in my car and clutched onto the pages. I pressed my thumb over one of the featured athletes' names, wedged inside a graphic sentence about being hooked. When I pictured my name there instead, the line felt just as true.

I leaned toward the rearview mirror. Dark circles had formed around my bloodshot eyes. My gums hurt from grinding my teeth. The shoulder lines on my winter coat slumped below my armpits. My pant legs grazed the floor mat. I had lost forty pounds within weeks. Twenty-nine-year-old Fred looked forty.

I reclined my seat and wept into the newsprint.

WHEN I GOT to work early the next day to tell Bob about my addiction, he was shocked. Mainly because I wasn't late for the first time in a while.

"Here's the deal," he told me. "This newsroom will welcome

you back to work. But we can't do that unless you take leave and get yourself help first."

He was talking about rehab. Inpatient rehab.

"Deal," I said. "But I want the public to know what's going on."

I had long considered myself a private person, but I proposed sharing for a few reasons. One was to stop false rumors from spreading during my upcoming time away. Another was the idea that talking about my recovery would make it more real. And perhaps a few struggling WDIV viewers would pursue their own sobriety, knowing that if the guy from TV was getting clean, so could they.

"I have a substance abuse problem, one that I must deal with, aided by those equipped to handle such difficulties on a clinical basis," I said in a statement to the Detroit papers. "I look forward to the day when I can say with pride that I have won this most personal of wars."

But before any victory day, I'd have to spend four weeks in a trench.

THE DIRECTOR at Greene Hall Rehabilitation Center in Xenia, Ohio, didn't mince words. I had been in the lobby for all of five minutes when he told me, "Those who don't get well will probably die of their disease."

He left no room for mystery, yet I still didn't understand. He seemed to be lumping me with the same strangers who were writhing and demanding one last fix down the hall. I didn't consider myself one of them. I told him that even if they were battling diseases, my case had more to do with bad decisions, not illness.

"Mr. Hickman," he said before showing me my room. "Everyone here is equal."

Staff recited Scripture. One counselor quoted Psalms 30:1-3:

"Oh, Lord, thou hast brought up my soul from the grave: Thou hast kept me alive, that I should not go down to the pit." Someone else read Matthew 11:28-30: "Come unto me, all ye that labor and are heavy laden, and I will give you rest." And James 5:15-16: "The prayer of faith shall save the sick."

The lines didn't resonate. Having grown up as an altar boy at a small Episcopal church in Springfield, I already knew the words. I wasn't impressed with where they had gotten me. I felt that by seeking God's help, I would be stealing His attention from the troubled souls whom I thought needed it more than I did.

Then came Movie Day. Just as I had done in elementary school whenever my teacher showed black-and-white snoozefests like *Health: Your Posture* or *Dental Hygiene: How and Why*, I strutted into the screening room with plans to nap.

Only this movie kept me wide awake. It was *Cocaine Blues*. To the sounds of out-of-sync piano keys and guitar twangs, it showed laboratory monkeys ignoring food and water—and choosing cocaine instead. The scene repeated so often, I thought the film reel was stuck, but no. Even as they were starving and dehydrating, the animals kept reaching for cocaine. They were picking fast, lively highs over life itself. Their decisions proved deadly.

No horror flick, not even as a kid, had made me shake the way this documentary did. After it ended, the other viewers left the room. But my legs were still too wobbly to stand back up, so I stayed seated. Once the space got quiet, I bowed my head. I placed my hands in my lap.

"Dear God, please help me."

He delivered.

I COMPLETED rehab and returned to Detroit, but not for long. It's not that I held hard feelings against the place; I just didn't want to reopen the trauma, darkness, or loneliness. Though I had only myself to blame for my addiction, sharing city limits with my former dealers would've done me no good. For all I knew, they may have thought I was a rat for telling the newspapers about my drug use. I had no desire to stick around and find out.

I wrote my resignation letter.

"In order for me to solve the personal problems in my life, a change of environment is mandatory," I wrote. "I must have the time and the freedom to deal with these problems. I cannot do so and provide the professional services that WDIV has contracted me to perform."

I handed Bob my notice, shook his hand, and went back to Springfield.

My childhood home felt safer for the time being. I stayed with Mom, caught up on the chores I had slacked off on as a kid, and mailed resumes to newsrooms across the country. I mowed the lawn almost every morning—way too often—so I could be near the mailbox in case job-related replies came. I dusted the family's old rotary phone so I could answer a future boss's call within one ring.

But I had no takers. The phone stayed silent. The mailman, who after a while knew what I was waiting for, shrugged and apologized.

I didn't regret getting clean, but I did start wishing I hadn't disclosed my problem. The very act that I had thought would broaden opportunities seemed to be narrowing them. I began to see the stigma that draws so many rehab graduates to relapse after rejoining society. Second to the effects of drug use and mental illness, the shame inflicted upon recovering souls is nothing I'd wish on my worst enemy.

The death of two promising talents that June almost broke me. University of Maryland star Len Bias, one of the greatest college basketball players I'd ever seen in person, died just two days after signing with the Boston Celtics. The twenty-two-year-old had used cocaine at a college party and, according to Maryland's chief medical examiner, suffered seizures and cardiac arrest within minutes. Eight days later, Cleveland Browns safety Don Rogers died of a cocaine overdose, aged twenty-three. In between prayers, for what felt like hours, I stared at newspaper images of Len smiling in his new Celtics hat—and of Don in uniform. They became shorthand for what-ifs.

But my first Narcotics Anonymous meeting helped me see the could-bes. A new generation of athletes could still find inspiration in the late ones' accomplishments. By listening to others and to myself, I could prevent more tragedy.

I began thanking God each morning for my second chance, though I suppose He had given me more than two by then. Over breakfast, as I began to regain the pounds cocaine had stolen, I thanked Him for empowering me to speak out about my addiction. For all my questions about whether I should or shouldn't have gone public about it, I finally came to appreciate this: He needed me to do it at exactly the moment I did—if not for me, then for someone else.

I made peace with the possibility that the broadcasting business would not welcome me back. Whatever came next, I would do it knowing I could finally offer a sounder mind.

The phone rang. I put down my cereal bowl and swallowed my mouthful of flakes.

"Hello?"

It was a producer from CNN. "How fast can you come back to Atlanta?"

I RETURNED to *Sports Tonight* that November. On my first day back, a higher-up who voted to rehire me told me who had swayed his decision. Nick had apparently told more than one executive that "Fred is worth the risk. Everybody deserves a second chance."

Maybe it was the recovering addict in me, but I was seeing lessons in everything and everyone, including in Nick. That he hadn't told me himself about how hard he'd vouched spoke volumes. He didn't want to make my return about himself, even if I couldn't have returned without him.

We jogged onto the set for our first show together in more than two years. Before I sat down, I turned to him.

"Thank you."

He paused. His eyes got glassy. He took a deep breath and cleared his throat.

"Welcome home."

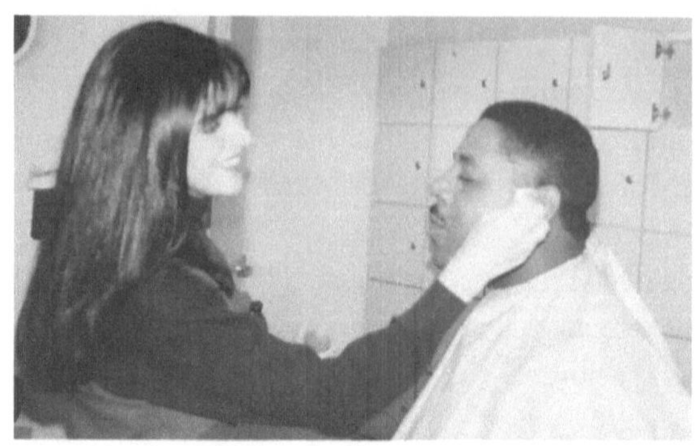

Makeup extraordinaire Rhonda Barrymore working her magic.

Covering Super Bowl XXIV in New Orleans.

With legendary CNN newsman Bernard Shaw.

6

AND WE'RE BACK

Even on the road, it felt as if I had never left CNN. Nick and I went to Los Angeles for our first CableACE Awards together. We knew the event would be a red-carpet affair, but only when we arrived did we realize how glitzy it would be. While everyone else pulled up in black stretch limousines, we putt-putted down the limo line with a red Ford Tempo from Hertz.

A passenger in a nearby limo rolled down her window. "Well, you guys certainly stand out."

Nick and I answered in unison. "We know!"

Rejoining *Sports Tonight* felt right. The bosses let me do more in-depth reporting, including a multi-part series on what was then a lack of Black head coaches in the National Football League. I tagged along with the 1988 Baltimore Orioles throughout their twenty-one-game losing streak; after the team's long-awaited victory, 9-0 over the Chicago White Sox, Nick swallowed his South Side pride and let me anchor a confetti-filled extravaganza. We sometimes hosted Saturday editions and would enjoy the booming, banging, crashing, and occasional "WOOOO!" coming from one floor above us—World Championship Wrestling matches.

"You know, I hear wrestling auditions are coming up," Nick told me once as we typed scripts. "You trying out?"

"Nah," I said. "Getting suplexed makes me dizzy."

Besides, I wanted I help people, not hurt them. I used whatever spare time I had to speak at rehab clinics, attend more Narcotics Anonymous meetings, and take calls from other recovering addicts. To watch good people work toward conquering their own demons was worth celebration.

There was plenty to celebrate. I've never followed ratings and wouldn't see the math until years later, but apparently within a year of my return, *Sports Tonight's* viewership jumped 75 percent, at times besting ESPN's *SportsCenter*. Maybe the viewers had missed me, or maybe more people were simply joining the cable bandwagon. Whatever the reason, being in their living rooms made me all the more grateful.

Ratings weren't all that grew. In 1987, CNN traded its original campus for a pair of fourteen-story office towers. Downtown Atlanta's newly christened CNN Center included a newsroom fit for what had become a 1,500-employee-strong network. Each desk had computers twice as fast as the ones we'd left behind. The days of punching Smith-Corona typewriter keys and praying for no typos were long gone. And after Ted Turner opened our new digs to daily public tours, I could simultaneously type and wave with ease.

Whenever a stranger asked where I worked, I'd usually say, "A shopping mall"—because that's what the complex's first few floors resembled. Trees in the atrium caught rays from high-up skylights. A sixplex theater screened films from the Metro-Goldwyn-Mayer library, which Ted had acquired a few years earlier. Full-service restaurants catered to workers and visitors alike. Sometimes in between meetings, I would sneak down for a burger and fries, which I'd eat while riding 196 feet up the world's longest free-standing escalator.

The steps rose quickly. So did our global profile.

. . .

ON THE NIGHT the Berlin Wall fell, someone in the newsroom shouted, "Fred! Look at the TV!" All I initially saw were hundreds of happy Germans at the Brandenburg Gate, some waving their flags, but then I looked closer. Live on a satellite feed, a reveler was holding up a bedsheet that read: "FRED ON CNN: UNITED GERMANY THE PLAY OF THE DAY."

My goodness, what a sight. Five minutes earlier, I would've doubted having any *Sports Tonight* viewers in East or West Germany, especially given all the turmoil there. But in that historic moment, I understood. Sports can offer a respite during divisive times. And at its best, sports can unite.

So by request, we included the German viewer's sign in that night's Play of the Day block, if only to show the world that Nick and I were here to stay.

WITH GLOBAL RECOGNITION came added responsibilities within the Turner Broadcasting family. When CNN's young sister channel Turner Network Television began airing professional basketball in 1989, I became a rotating host for a new in-studio postgame program that has since reached new heights. We called it *Inside the NBA*.

The show launched as more of a highlights rundown than anything. Think of it as an all-hoops spin on *Sports Tonight*. It certainly wasn't the laugh-out-loud parade that Ernie Johnson Jr., Kenny Smith, Charles Barkley, and Shaquille O'Neal would later craft it into so well, but I still enjoyed my five or so years on *Inside*. I mean, how could I *not* enjoy spending a half-hour saying the names of Jordan, Scottie, Bird, Magic, Isiah, Olajuwon, Dominique, Sir Charles, The Glide, The Mailman, and The Admiral?

Also on my list of extracurricular activities was football. In

1990, the NFL stretched *Sunday Night Football* to sixteen weeks, giving ESPN the second half and TNT the first. For me, that meant manning eight one-hour pregame shows a year. And because we liked one-upping ESPN, I hosted not in a studio but at each game site. Watching stadiums rise from dead-quiet to Richter-grade by playtime made my blood feel electric.

NFL offseasons gave me more chances to see sports at their best. Along with the 1990 Goodwill Games in Seattle and the 1992 Winter Olympics in Albertville, France, the 1994 games will always be one of my favorite examples. I know many crowds understandably associate 1994 with the vicious attack on ice skater Nancy Kerrigan, but what also stood out to me was the overall hope for world peace. In welcoming sixty-seven nations to Lillehammer—where Israeli intelligence officers had killed the wrong man while pursuing a suspect in the 1972 Munich kidnapping two decades earlier—the small Norwegian town committed itself to bridge-building. Thanks to a deal between CBS and TNT, we got in on some of the coverage.

Literal highs replaced my chemical ones. From the roof of a floating hotel, Nick and I hosted coverage of the 1994 Goodwill Games in St. Petersburg, Russia. I'd never expected to visit a country that had been so curtained for so long, but there I was, an American sitting hundreds of feet above the Gulf of Finland, Saint Isaac's Cathedral, the Winter Palace, and two thousand athletes from around the world. Everyone below us looked bug-sized. At night, with our bright camera lights, every flying bug in Russia attacked us.

All that fly-shooing made me hungry. After a particularly busy night—or early morning, depending on who you ask—the hotel's head chef asked me what I wanted to eat. I told him just a plain old hamburger would do. Minutes later, a waiter handed me a meatball slapped between two wet slices of bread. Yeah, it looked more like something Gaylord Perry would've thrown at ninety miles an hour, but the chef's toothy smile as he awaited my bite showed such unshakable joy. He took pride in his craft. I couldn't resist that.

And you know what? The burger wound up tasting pretty darn good. Wherever that chef is now, I want to tell him, "Spasibo."

TRAVELING the world offers the best chance to see how small it is. At a convention in Las Vegas, I spotted the news director from Waterloo, Iowa. This was the one who had told me more than a decade earlier that his TV station wasn't ready to hire a journalist of color. We made eye contact.

I smiled. "Are you ready now?"

He laughed. "I am if you are."

"Thanks. But come to think of it, I'm happy where I am."

The early-'90s-era CNN Sports team, with ringmaster Bill MacPhail in the center.

Preparing for the launch of CNN/SI, a twenty-four-hour sports news channel.

The dynamic duo.

7

EXPANSION

Because I hadn't wreaked enough havoc playing high school basketball, some cable industry bigwigs handpicked me to give Major League Baseball a try. These important people somehow theorized that by watching me toss the first pitch at a Florida Marlins game, Greater Miami's many elders would finally decide en masse to trade their rabbit ears for cable boxes.

Big mistake. I threw a slider that accidentally whacked the catcher, who in this case was team mascot Billy the Marlin. The ball nailed that big head of his. He fell beak-first onto the dirt. I walked to home plate to apologize and shake hands, but all I got was Billy cursing under his breath. Security rushed me off the field. That was that.

Whenever anyone asks me what cable TV was like in the 1990s, I use Billy's injury as a metaphor. We all should have worn helmets.

CNN's coverage of the Persian Gulf War introduced live combat into American living rooms in 1991. An exclusive deal with Iraqi television allowed correspondents to file unedited play-by-play over the phone from Baghdad's Al-Rashid Hotel. Bernard Shaw, John Holliman, and Peter Arnett crouched under beds and tables as they detailed the ongoing neon flashes. But rawest of all were the real-time booms of anti-aircraft fire. No other shop—not ABC, CBS, or NBC—had the time or resources of America's lone twenty-four-hour news channel. In record numbers, households feasted on the nonstop media cycle that would color all the big stories to come.

Though *Sports Tonight* didn't cover the war, and was often preempted on the nights of more newsworthy battles, our program stayed alive. Ratings remained solid whenever we did air. Nick and I were still having fun. A few years after the war, long after we had regained our usual time slot, a CNN promotions person approached the two of us with breaking news: We were about to anchor our three thousandth show together.

I spun in my office chair, toward Nick. "Who's even got the time to count that?"

"Or the patience!" he replied.

"Funny. We never set out to break records. Yet here we are."

"Maybe that's the beauty of it."

Despite our milestone, competition was building. ESPN's *SportsCenter* had upped its offensive by turning our former CNN colleagues Keith Olbermann and Dan Patrick into a rival eleven p.m. tag team. Worst of all, the two were fantastic, as I'd predicted. Dan's guy-next-door reliability and Keith's transgressive jousting tested the limits of hot and cool. Pickup basketball games were no longer complete without at least one participant quoting a Dan catchphrase: "Dare I say, en fuego." And because of a photographic mind that could stuff ABBA, Abbott and Costello, and Bella Abzug references into a single breath, another Dan-ism easily applied to Keith: "You can't stop him, you can only hope to contain him." Their potential to trounce *Sports Tonight* seemed as boundless as their scripts and ad-libs. One columnist went so far as to write in 1994, "They are the best tandem act since the heyday of Nick and Hick in the 1980s."

Nick and I kept going nonetheless. We continued trekking to assignments, scoring exclusive one-on-ones, and hunting for Plays of the Day as usual. *Sports Illustrated* ran a profile about our lasting "TV marriage," calling us the "best-dressed" and "best-meshed" late-night sports duo. And with ESPN's growing menu of live baseball, football, hockey, and college games often delaying the Keith and Dan show, the CNN promo team marketed us as the more punctual pair.

We at *Sports Tonight* thought CNN's broader viewer base would still distinguish us from *SportsCenter's* usual boys' club. We clung to our mission of producing a sports roundup for all. If ESPN—the so-called "Worldwide Leader in Sports"—had what its chief anchors nicknamed "The Big Show," we at "The Most Trusted Name in News" had "The Big Tent." One of the best compliments I kept receiving was "I didn't like sports much until I started watching you and Nick."

We planned a busy show on Friday, June 17, 1994. Earlier that day, Arnold Palmer had taken his final bow at golf's U.S. Open. The first World Cup on U.S. soil had just kicked off. The New York Rangers had paraded down Broadway, celebrating their first Stanley Cup in fifty-four years. I was covering Game Five of the NBA Finals.

But an unscripted soap opera involving an NFL steamroller would overhaul everything.

THE OPENING ACT had the live viewership of a Super Bowl. Some ninety-five million Americans watched aerial video, on CNN or elsewhere, as O. J. Simpson evaded Los Angeles police from the back of a former teammate's moving white Ford Bronco. The legendary running back, *Naked Gun* actor, and smiley Hertz pitchman—accused of killing his wife and her male friend—held a gun to his own head for the better part of two hours. Viewers wondered if this cultural icon would die by suicide on live television. Crowds cheered from freeway overpasses, telling one of America's fastest men to outrun the blue and red lights. Then at 8:47 p.m. Pacific time, officers declared their manhunt over; O. J. had surrendered outside his Brentwood mansion, and nonstop coverage had blazed through *Sports Tonight's* thirty-minute slot.

The subsequent trial once again showed CNN's power to take a single story, go wall-to-wall, and score big. Over 133 days, courtroom camera feeds lent instant access to the arguments, the testimony, and a dynamic cast. Judge Lance Ito, prosecutor Marcia Clark, LAPD detective Mark Fuhrman, aspiring actor Kato Kaelin, and "Dream Team" defenders Johnnie Cochran, Robert Shapiro, Alan Dershowitz, and Robert Kardashian each became household names. Transcripts became the stuff of murder mysteries, racial inquiry, and Hollywood gossip. So by the time the real jury declared O. J. not guilty in October 1995, many CNN viewers had come to feel like jurors themselves.

Some amateur analysts declared the trial a victory for our channel. They said that despite Court TV also airing the case in full, CNN had captured a wider audience—and was available in three times as many homes. They claimed ESPN had dropped the ball by not inflating the sports angle enough. A few brave souls even predicted CNN would hold a lasting monopoly on 24/7 news.

Jinx.

Not only did the opposite come true. New competitors in 1996 hit *Sports Tonight* from all sides.

Take cable news, for one. MSNBC and Fox News Channel launched under the growing post-trial belief that day-in-day-out coverage (or at least commentary) was finally a lucrative enough mine to raid. With each day, MSNBC's techiness and Fox's punchiness gnawed at CNN's market share.

On top of that, a sports media schism cost us even more viewers. Fox Sports Net premiered with its own nightly show, *Fox*

Sports News. ESPN unleashed a spinoff channel called ESPNews, which gave scores on a big ticker and highlights on a thirty-minute wheel. And a new thing called the internet allowed fans to track out-of-town scores and headlines in real time, without *Sports Tonight* or TV at all.

The piling challenges led an intern, a college kid, to approach me and Nick one night.

"Where'll this business even be in a few years?" he asked.

"Lots of new places, but the fundamentals won't change," Nick told him before referencing one of my favorite *I Love Lucy* scenes. "Fred and I will just have to keep scooping up the candy."

And throughout what would be our final months sharing the *Sports Tonight* desk, that's what we did.

MANAGEMENT SPLIT me and Nick up in 1997. I loathed the idea. It led more than a few probably well-meaning folks to tell me in the hall, "All great things must come to an end." I rolled my eyes so many times, my optometrist had to prescribe me thicker lenses.

The higher-ups spelled out their reason: CNN/SI. Born from Time Warner's 1996 purchase of Turner Broadcasting, this was their dream of an all-sports news channel that would do what rivals couldn't. While ESPN and Fox Sports were filling more and more hours with live sporting events, this new venture would spend that time breaking big stories. It would mesh CNN's on-air might with *Sports Illustrated* magazine's in-depth reporting. It would outdo ESPNews with nineteen live hours a day. Shows would include a revamped *Sports Tonight*—which would be simulcast on the original CNN channel and star yours truly—and an hour-long newsmagazine hosted by Nick.

For me, the change brought initial swings and misses. I accidentally referred to my new coanchor, Vince Cellini, as "Nick" on air. We lost more ground to *SportsCenter*. Hoping to liven things up, I asked one of the new CNN/SI execs if we could do a few shows from Atlanta's new Official All-Star Café, part of a sports-themed restaurant chain from investors Andre Agassi, Wayne Gretzky, Ken Griffey Jr., Joe Montana, Shaquille O'Neal, and Monica Seles. Months after my proposal's rejection, ESPN opened a similar joint called the ESPN Zone and began hosting shows there. Go figure.

But for all my struggles, I enjoyed seeing Nick branch out. His program, *Page One*, let him go beyond the usual fifteen-second interview clips and two-minute packages. He could go longer on deeper issues. He could finally fill his black notepad with exclusives he wouldn't have gotten by staying put.

Watching my friend do his thing made me imagine what else I could do. And compared to my mistakes of long ago, my mind was now in a healthier place to explore.

MY HOUSE WAS GROWING. I had a wife, Judy. We had a son named Mack and later a daughter, Gabrielle. More than thirty years after my father showed me his workplace, I started taking my kids to mine. I would sit down, clip on my studio mic, and talk. More clearly than ever, I'd hear hints of the late George Hickman's voice in my own.

Troubling events left me concerned about my children's generation. Five minutes after finishing interviews at the 1996 Olympics in Atlanta, a pipe bomb exploded near the exact spot where I had stood for hours. I couldn't stop thinking about the woman killed in this domestic terrorist attack, the family milestones she would miss, and the families of more than one hundred injured people. Not to mention other sports stories emerging around then, of major athletes spitting on umpires, choking coaches, or committing sex crimes. Though *Sports Tonight* had a duty to cover each of these issues, I didn't want viewers of any age to come away hating sports as a result.

As I brainstormed ways to share more inspiring sports stories, I thought of my interview with Michael Jordan from earlier that year, which just happened to have fallen on Father's Day. Michael had led the Chicago Bulls to an NBA title minutes before our chat, capping his first full season back in basketball since his father's death. He had wiped tears from his face and said of the late James Jordan, "He's been with me all season long. Ever since he's been gone, he's been in my heart."

And what a heart it is.

So *More Than a Game* was born. It debuted in 1997 as a syndicated weekly half-hour newsmagazine, allowing me to cover the humanity in sports. I'll never forget how Travis Roy, who had sustained a back-breaking injury eleven seconds into his Boston College hockey career, created a multimillion-dollar foundation for spinal research. Nor will I forget California high school basketball coach Ken Carter, who suspended his whole team for two games after players cut class. Or eleven-year-old Jason Duncan, who in 1998 caught a Mark McGwire home run, found McGwire after the game, and handed the ball back to the slugger as a gift. I can only hope my many guests had as much fun being on as I did featuring them over the course of four years.

The feel-good show felt like my good luck charm. I left each taping and assignment smiling more. Even when my Monday-through-Friday job at CNN/SI forced me to handle the darker side of sports, I sighed less. And young Mack, whom I'd taken on a few shoots, started asking me to play sports with him. Hoops in our driveway. Catch in our backyard. A father's dreams.

Then came a reporter's dream assignment. As the year 2000 approached, CNN president Rick Kaplan offered me a plane ticket to New York. It wasn't to cover a sporting event, though a ball and crowd were involved.

"New Year's Eve. Times Square," Rick told me. "You in?"

Damn right, I was. I didn't buy into all the doomsday talk about Y2K causing power grids to fail, currencies to collapse, nuclear warheads to fire themselves, planes to fall from the sky, and

VCRs to blink zeroes forever. I figured that even in the rare case of such chaos, Times Square would offer some of the planet's tightest security.

I was right. In the leadup to midnight, the place resembled a human cocoon. Eight thousand NYPD officers were stationed in Times Square alone. Manhole covers were welded shut. Two million celebrants sardined themselves between 34th Street and 59th, between Sixth Avenue and Eighth. All were there to watch the same 1,070-pound Waterford crystal ball drop seventy-seven feet toward a sign that would flash "2000." A combination of body heat, neon lights, and seven thousand gallons of donated coffee warmed everyone up in the freezing cold. Not even I, who'd spent almost twenty years at CNN reporting on shared cultural experiences, had seen one like this before.

Surely enough, the new year came without a hitch. Fireworks shot from One Times Square. Three thousand pounds of confetti rained on us. Relieved strangers hugged. Excited sweethearts kissed. "Auld Lang Syne" blasted from the speakers. And somehow through the overpowering cheers and hallelujahs, I still heard my cue to deliver one of CNN's first live remarks of the new era:

> Isn't it a wonderful thing? You have two million people. Two million people compressed into this small area here in Midtown Manhattan. No incidents. And it's just been a loving experience for everybody involved here. Spirits are so high.
>
> My hope for the new year, for all of us, is that we can continue on with that good feeling and carry it into other areas of our lives and perhaps enjoy ourselves a lot more than the last one thousand years. We should do this again in 3000.

Even the cleanup amazed me. By the time I left Times Square at around two a.m., most of the revelers were gone, and the blocks where they had gathered were quiet. The only sound left was the hum of garbage trucks and street sweepers. All in a night's work.

I awoke at seven o'clock in my hotel room. I walked a few blocks, back to the scene of the party. No more confetti. No more trash. Hardly any sign that one of mankind's largest-ever gatherings had happened there mere hours earlier. Just a society that kept moving.

Life goes on. It's a cliché, but it's true. It keeps me humble after good changes—and grateful after bad.

8

ME, MYSELF, AND IVERSON

To anyone who skipped right to this chapter without reading anything before it, I welcome you to this wild ride.

Yes, the 2000 election overtook my life. It dominated cable TV. It left talk radio switchboards buzzing, columnists fuming, and readers mailing angry letters. Whether I was working or at home on the phone, it was all anyone wanted to grill me on. Even after I voted, the uproar over the final tally wasn't stopping. After a while, it made me question my and my family's safety. To this day, it's still a heated topic among buffs.

And no, I'm not referring to a presidential race.

Shaquille O'Neal's 1999-2000 campaign was as intimidating as the seven-foot-one, 315-pound center himself. In each game that season, he averaged a league-high 29.7 points on 57.4 percent shooting, 13.6 rebounds, 3.03 blocks, and a career-high 3.8 assists. With his rap and movie side gigs drawing more eyes to the hardwood, he led the Los Angeles Lakers to a 67-15 record, second-best in team history.

That's why he almost became the league's first-ever unanimously elected Most Valuable Player. As I would learn, 120 of 121 league writers and broadcasters voted for him that spring.

All but one. Me.

My vote came down to a question: Which player had raised his team's value the most? To cast my ballot, I had a pen, highlighter, calculator, and eight months of newspaper clippings and box scores. Remove Shaq from those Lakers, and chances are Kobe Bryant's 22.5 points per game and Glen Rice's 15.9 would have still helped that club go far. As much as I would have picked Shaq for any fantasy team or a Player of the Year category, my gut told me he could only be my runner-up for MVP. My first choice was someone else.

I answered "The Answer." Allen Iverson's return from a broken thumb had lifted the Philadelphia 76ers from .500 ball to a 38-22 record for the rest of the season. His average of 28.4 points per game that year bested those of Tyrone Hill and Theo Ratliff combined, while his 2.1 steals per game cracked the league's top five. He held steady at the free-throw line and sank eighty-nine threes, more than Aaron McKie, George Lynch, and a post-trade Toni Kukoč combined. And at six feet tall, he had turned being one of the game's shorter players into a strength, sliding through the opposition's defensive holes. Sure, the Sixers fell in the second round, but without their guard, they may not have met a winning season let alone a postseason. While L.A. boasted myriad freeways to success, Philly's relevance that year had just one spelling: A. I.

So I mailed my sealed ballot. Destination: Fifth Avenue, New York, New York, where NBA officials about a dozen stories high promised never to disclose who had voted for whom.

What I got in return was anything but secret.

My agent, Lou, called a few mornings later to ask if I was ready for a crazy day. I asked him what he meant.

"You voted for Iverson," he said.

Um . . . "How do you know?" I asked.

"*L.A. Times.* The whole world knows. All the others wrote in Shaq. You've pissed everyone off."

"Everyone?"

"Well, everyone but Iverson."

I was home and ran to my computer. I checked LATimes.com. There it was: *"According to one source, CNN sports anchor Fred Hickman denied O'Neal the unanimous tally by giving Philadelphia 76er guard Allen Iverson his first-place vote."*

At least I had already dropped my son off at school. Otherwise he would've overheard his pops yelling some not-nice words.

By the time I got to work that afternoon, I couldn't even use the bathroom without someone demanding an explanation. I fielded questions from radio stations, websites, newspapers, and a newsstand cashier. Even on his Los Angeles radio show, former MTV veejay André "Doctor Dré" Brown asked what the hell I was thinking.

I spent hours giving the same responses. Over and over, I said this was not a suicide mission against a legend nor a ploy for headlines. How was I supposed to predict that all the other voters would, for the first time in NBA history, back the same guy for MVP? How could I have been seeking fame by submitting what was meant to be a secret ballot? I wasn't threatening anyone's existence. I wasn't out to get anyone. I didn't want to spark another Spanish Inquisition. I was just voting my conscience. That was it.

Some two dozen interviews later, I went on *Sports Tonight* that night hoisting up an "O'Neal 34" jersey. I wanted to show I hardly hated the guy. My exact words on that night's show were for him: "I love you, man. Don't hit me."

Later that night at the Lakers' El Segundo practice facility, Shaq got his Maurice Podoloff Trophy and seemed to brush off the whole ordeal. "I'd like to thank everyone who voted for me," he said before flashing a smile. "And the one guy who didn't, thank you too. I appreciate it."

Everyone near him exploded in laughter. So did I when a reporter at the scene told me about it over the phone. I was glad Shaq had brought it up. The air was clear. We'd had our humor. Now let's move on.

Yet so many people acted like I had killed the president or kidnapped the Lindbergh baby. Lakers vice president (and living NBA silhouette) Jerry West told reporters regarding the vote, "God, I feel sorry for the one guy who didn't vote for him." Lakers forward Robert Horry doubled down, saying, "I heard some guy at CNN didn't vote for him. Did he ever play?" A coworker approached my desk and showed me what a beloved *Boston Globe* columnist had written: "Face it, Freddy. You've made a fool out of yourself for all sports eternity."

I had never gotten so much grief over anything. More people took jabs against me than explained why they disagreed. With very few exceptions, nobody seemed interested in rational debate or conversation. Just yelling.

At one point, while still at work, I made the mistake of channel-surfing. "For Fred Hickman not to vote for Shaquille O'Neal is one of two things," one commentator said, "either a publicity stunt or total ignorance for the game of basketball." Another tried joking that Iverson's crew must have my young daughter "tied up in a Brooklyn basement" and "there was some extortion going on."

Alright, enough cheap shots. Quip about me all you want, but family is off limits. I turned off my desktop TV and walked out.

The moment I got home, sometime after two a.m., I checked on Gabby and Mack. Both were sound asleep in their beds. No extortion. No basements. No tied limbs.

I turned off my cell phone and tried to fall asleep.

When I got to the CNN Center the next day, the answering machine at my desk blinked more digits than ever. I hit play. We had a problem.

"You'd better watch your back."

"You ain't seen nothing yet."

"If your ass ever comes to Los Angeles again, you're never getting out."

I ignored the voicemails until I couldn't. As I stood in the Kroger checkout line that Sunday with Mack, a cashier told me, "You're gonna be assassinated." Rather than making a scene or getting violent in front of a seven-year-old, I took my son and slowly backed out of the line. We restocked the items in our cart and took our business elsewhere.

At work that Monday, I ejected the anger-laced tape from my answering machine. I headed straight to the corner office. We had to do something.

The bosses inside reached two conclusions. First, security guards were going to follow me around until things settled down. Second, if Shaq's Lakers made the NBA Finals, I would be safer not covering them in L.A.

Indeed, the Lakers did make it. They eclipsed the Phoenix Suns in five games then edged out the Portland Trail Blazers in seven. In Game Six of the Finals, Shaq nailed an off-kilter shot that blew the Indiana Pacers away for good. Los Angeles grabbed its first crown since 1988, its first of three straight titles.

Sometime after watching the celebration on a newsroom TV, I stretched my legs and saw one of the CNN security guards. It was one of the burly guys who, after the phone threats, had promised I would be alright. His deep voice felt reassuring.

"I've gotta praise you, man," he told me. "The folks'll see that you've stuck to your guns. Just wait."

Part of me hoped so. Still, hearing it from someone else didn't hurt.

IT TOOK A FEW WEEKS, but the hysteria finally waned. And

almost exactly a year later, in May 2001, an MVP Award went to none other than Allen Ezail Iverson.

This time, I got another nickname. A nicer one.

"Yo, Nostradamus!" someone in the CNN lobby shouted one afternoon right before my shift.

Iverson's powerful 2000-01 season led some people to think more highly of my 2000 ballot. The same critics who had called me a contrarian attention-grabber were now saying I'd delivered a spot-on prediction. Others suggested my vote had planted the idea of Iverson as MVP into my fellow voters' heads (though such a statement doesn't give the player enough credit). "People said he was crazy . . . outlandish . . . just plain wrong," one columnist wrote. "Could it be that Fred Hickman was merely a year early?"

"Feeling vindicated yet?" a sportswriter asked me.

I jokingly said yes. In truth, not even close.

Frustrated was more like it. That nobody in the NBA office had denounced the leak baffled me. For all the public outcry over who I had or hadn't voted for, the fact that someone had mishandled my ballot didn't seem to concern any officials. As far as I know, none showed interest in finding the person responsible. None set out to avoid future privacy breaches. If the league's suits haven't learned their lesson yet, I hope they will someday.

I didn't let myself admit it then, but yeah, the whole Shaq saga did embitter me for a time. It showed me how the noise of talk radio was bleeding into journalism spaces. Sports television was becoming less about storytelling and interviewing and more about pundits arguing. You had to be ready to stop and yell (or be yelled at) over anything at all times: basketball, politics, the shape of Earth. If enough people disagreed with your opinion—or worse, basic facts—you had to brace for threats, even if your views weren't demeaning, dehumanizing, or brainwashing anyone. Bad precedents were emerging.

But through my sourness, I did find aspects to appreciate. The fiasco deepened my empathy for the sports world's scapegoats. I gained more empathy for Bill Buckner, a skilled first baseman mistreated after a grounder rolled through his legs during the 1986 World Series. After the 2003 National League Championship Series, I couldn't help but feel for my fellow Cubs fan Steve Bartman, whom many suspect cost the team a pennant by deflecting a fly ball in foul territory; Bartman wound up getting police protection because of it. It's not my place to compare my situation to theirs, but I did come to see that they deserved better.

Believe it or not, this whole mess also reaffirmed my civic pride. It helped me teach my kids to stand up for their values—and to let others peacefully speak theirs. I'm glad to live in a country that protects voter anonymity, at least in government elections. I'm grateful for the ancestors who fought against jelly bean tests so I can vote. I vowed never to skip so much as a primary or down-ballot race again.

Being an American is a responsibility. That will always be so, especially in tragedy.

9

PAUSE

Another chapter in a legend's life was beginning. Standing near the curb outside his Chicago restaurant on a Monday night, thirty-eight-year-old Michael Jordan all but confirmed it to my colleague Marty Burns. Three years into his second retirement, the longtime Chicago Bull was ready to lace up his Nikes once again, this time with the Washington Wizards. He told Marty and two other reporters, "I'm doing it for the love of the game. Nothing else."

This was easily the top story. Early into that night's *Sports Tonight*, Marty told me more about his conversation, saying Michael seemed less focused on winning a seventh championship and more devoted to mentoring younger teammates. Vince Cellini did a piece on how a return would likely boost NBA attendance and viewership, both of which had dipped since Michael's 1998 farewell. Then to end the show, I told viewers they could expect Michael to officialize his comeback at a news conference within ten days.

But a lot can happen in ten days. Executives can gut offices. Familiar faces can disappear. An employee who has watched an underdog newsroom become a global brand can decide it's okay to say goodbye.

Heck, forget ten days. A lot can happen in ten hours.

AT 9:03 a.m. the next day—Tuesday, September 11, 2001—I could've sworn I was watching a replay. The newscast on my living room TV showed a plane hitting New York's World Trade Center. An anchor said a plane had hit one of the complex's towers seventeen minutes earlier, so I assumed that's what I was looking at.

Only it was no replay. It was live. A second plane. A second tower. A second plume of smoke. And as a licensed pilot who had flown private jets every so often, I could tell this was no accident.

If the New York hijackings didn't confirm that this was war, crashes later that morning at the Pentagon and in rural Pennsylvania did. The more I flipped between CNN, MSNBC, ABC, CBS, NBC, and Fox, the more I feared that Atlanta—home of the world's busiest airport by passenger traffic—would be the next terror site.

I grabbed my keys and drove. Whatever was coming, I wanted Mack home with Judy and Gabby. So I picked him up at school.

The drive back to our house was near-silent. I would normally hear all sorts of planes come and go above me, but not this time. The federal government had grounded all private and commercial flights. The only sounds were of fighter jets circling Dobbins Air Reserve Base—and of me telling Mack as we entered our driveway, "We're home, kiddo."

Little did I know, I was about to spend a lot more time at home.

THERE WAS no *Sports Tonight* that night. In its place, CNN continued its rolling coverage of the hijackings. Even the all-sports CNN/SI, which would normally air our show regardless of hard-news events, stuck with a full simulcast of CNN. After all, pretty much every American sports league had decided earlier that day to postpone the rest of the week's games. This was, understandably, no time to play.

So when a bunch of AOL Time Warner higher-ups brought me into a conference room the next day and said, "We're taking *Sports Tonight* off CNN's schedule," I figured they meant until the following Monday.

Then a guy in a suit corrected me. "No. Off for good."

And that was it. The CNN staple that had existed since the channel's earliest days—which had given me chances to travel far, make close friends, and build the life I knew—was muzzled. Though the show would stay on CNN/SI, the corporate executives didn't sound hopeful about the little-watched spinoff channel's future. I would learn that ten of my colleagues would be laid off by the end of that week alone. As the prospect of war loomed over the country, America's longest-running cable news network was losing its two-decade-old appetite for sports journalism.

"We're giving you a choice," a boss told me. "Stay with the company in some capacity. Or resign, and we'll pay out your contract."

"If I stay in some capacity, what capacity would that be?"

Nobody spoke. Meanwhile, two or three security guards looked into the conference room through a glass divide. They stared at me like I was going to spray the place with bullets.

I broke the awkward silence with more pointed question. "Would I still do sports?"

"Not necessarily."

"News?"

"Not sure yet."

"Domestic or overseas?"

"We don't know. Even if we did know, we can't talk about it."

I looked back out at the guards. They were still guarding.

Another executive spoke from the corner of the room. "We

need to know whether you plan to stay or quit by the end of today."

Journalism is all about deadlines. That day, it involved deciding the future of my own career in eight hours or less. So just as I had with all my CNN assignments over the years, I trusted my gut.

"I'll take my check and go."

On my way out the door, I called my agent. "Lou, it's time."

I WAS GONE from the CNN family but apparently not forgotten. A few days after I quit, some creative CNN/SI staffers emailed me photos of a full-size Fred Hickman replica they had made beside my old newsroom desk. They used papier-mâché for my head and brown duct tape for my skin. They fit a leftover white button-down over my chair, for my body, and tucked a Dunkin' Donuts napkin into the shirt collar. They used black tape for my hair, mustache, and brows. Real headphones on each ear. An untied turquoise tie around my neck. A bottle of baby oil and an empty yogurt container near my old computer. Covering the desktop keyboard was a note for the cleaning crew: "DO NOT TAKE." The only things missing were burning candles and Gregorian chants.

I missed many of my former comrades—and got a kick out of their shrine—but I still didn't regret leaving. The previous twelve months or so had brought the departures of CNN mainstays: Elsa Klensch, Bobbie Battista, Frank Sesno, president Rick Kaplan, and my friends Nick Charles and Bernie Shaw. Another founding anchor, Lou Waters, left later that month. A phone call with Bernie around that time gave me perspective: "Your kids are only kids once, Fred. Savor the moments."

Savor we did. Gabby and I went out for ice cream. Mack and I played more catch and practiced our golf swings. And when the appropriate time came for sports to resume, I got to watch at home with my family. Instead of rushing to clip and write highlights for a show, I poured chips into a big bowl for us all to share. I knew I'd go back into broadcasting at some point, but until then, being a viewer in a comfy couch rejuvenated me.

We sat in awe as two events in New York, on the same October night, showed how sports can comfort a hurting nation. TBS had Michael Jordan's first game back, which happened to be against the Knicks in Madison Square Garden; a sellout crowd welcomed Michael, who'd decided to give his year's salary to 9/11 relief efforts. Over on Fox, before Game Three of the World Series between the New York Yankees and Arizona Diamondbacks, President George W. Bush stepped onto the Yankee Stadium pitcher's mound, gave a thumbs-up, and threw a perfect strike. No war could steal our games.

And as fortune would have it, my agent soon called to deliver four words I never thought I'd hear.

"The Yankees want you."

(P. S.: CNN/SI closed shop that May, citing low availability and even lower viewership. Though most of the sports news channel's two hundred employees were laid off, the papier-mâché replica of me remained. A former colleague somehow stuffed the thing into a wall. No matter where I go, I guess you can say I'll forever be part of CNN's wall-to-wall coverage.)

The life-size Fred Hickman replica.

On the YES set with former CNN/SI mates Brian Tees (center) and Jeff "Quags" Quagliata (right). Quags became the research manager at YES.

With Gabby (left) and Mack (right).

10

YES MAN

Conventional wisdom suggested I didn't belong. The New York Yankees were baseball's wealthiest and winningest club, having amassed thirty-eight pennants and twenty-six World Series titles by that point. I was a Chicago Cubs fan who had spent his whole life insulting billy goats, browsing clearance racks, and watching his team lose. The idea of the Yankees wanting anything to do with me made no sense.

But neither I nor the Yankees cared. Ahead of the 2002 baseball season, the team named me a studio host for its new self-owned cable channel, the Yankees Entertainment and Sports Network, or YES. I would be the face of its shows: the pregame, the postgame, and the weekly *Yankees Magazine*. I'd interview prospects, Hall of Famers, and players in between. Even for a Cubs fan, having this much access to the storied Yankees was a gift from the baseball and journalism gods. Plus I would host pregames and postgames for basketball's New Jersey Nets. My new boss, executive producer John J. Filippelli, figured that having a CNN original at the YES desk would bring familiarity to this not-yet-familiar channel.

Still, the job had initial bumps. After mentioning Yankees

pitcher David Wells's recent two-year, $7 million Yankees contract, I got a call on my office phone. Without introduction, the caller got right to yelling—"Hitchcock! We never mention player salaries! Never again!"—then hung up.

Had the caller not confused my last name with that of Yankees pitcher Sterling Hitchcock, I would've thought he was team owner George Steinbrenner. The fast staccato delivery had sounded just like him.

"You won't believe the crank call I just got," I told John minutes later. "The guy's Steinbrenner impression was spot on!"

"It wasn't a crank," he said. "It was George. He told me the same thing a little while ago."

Whoops.

Another early issue involved carriage. A clash with the provider Cablevision left YES, with its majority of Yankees games, unavailable to millions of Tri-State customers for the entire 2002 season. Angry callers rang often.

One person who did have access to YES was a New York state trooper. He spotted me one afternoon on Interstate 95 zooming faster than I should've in my new BMW convertible. His lights and siren went on. I pulled over, as did he.

"Hey, you're the Yankees guy, aren't you?" he asked.

"Yeah, I'm very sorry, sir," I told him. "I was actually running late to work. That's why I was speeding."

I opened the glove box, where I kept my registration and insurance cards. I handed him everything he requested and put my hands atop the steering wheel.

He glanced over my registration but quickly lost interest. Something else in the box caught his attention.

"You know," he said, "I like the Yankees."

"Oh yeah? Me too."

"No. I *really* like the Yankees."

The trooper winked and pointed at the glove box. It turned out I had been so busy trying to keep my hands in plain sight, to avoid rash escalation, that I'd forgotten to close the compartment. He must have seen the Yankees season-ticket book I kept in there. The tickets were a perk of my job, but I was usually too busy working to use them myself.

"I *love* Yankee Stadium," the trooper said, sticking his neck forward. "In fact, my shift ends about an hour before tonight's first pitch."

He made it clear that he wouldn't leave without game tickets. So I slipped a pair his way. He took them and sped off.

I suppose the stop could've ended far worse.

I WANTED the perfect life for my family, which meant buying the perfect house. I found it in Scarsdale, a lush New York suburb eighteen miles north of Yankee Stadium and eighteen miles west of YES's Stamford, Connecticut, studio. Its windows lent views of rolling green hills and towering trees. Its interior offered a play-room for the kids and a basement office for me. A big living room allowed Mack and Gabby to host all their new friends.

But the home's best features had nothing to do with luxury. Wide hallways and ramps helped my wife, Judy, get around more easily. It was the least she deserved as her years-long battle with multiple sclerosis began making movement an increasingly hard task. This place, at this point in our lives, was her best hope at tackling each day as best she could. We didn't stop making each day as memorable as possible.

When it came to building memories in Scarsdale, we felt like royalty. A store called Big Top spared us from the yearly mayhem of back-to-school shopping, offering huge prepackaged bags with every supply the kids could need. Thanks to our house's proximity to Quaker Ridge Elementary School, Judy and I would exhale watching Mack walk straight into class from our porch. On my days or nights off, we'd go to an ice cream shop named Last Licks, which doubled as a goldmine for signed baseballs and other sports memorabilia. On late work nights, I'd simply grab a phone, say my name, and this one diner would have my corned beef hash, sliced pie, and cornbread ready by the time I reached the Westchester County line. And home deliveries of groceries made life easier when Judy was in too much pain to leave the house.

Scarsdale Little League gave the kids a distraction from their mother's illness. They thought it was so cool that each team shared a major-league club's name. It made them feel like pros, especially in our family town.

Gabby was the only girl on the Devil Rays. I was so excited. The day she joined the team, I bought her a glove with velcro bands, thinking it would stay on her hand better during a play. But one afternoon in the bleachers, I looked toward the outfield grass and saw her sitting, gloveless, and picking flowers. I don't even know where the glove was. She couldn't have cared less about actually playing, but the joy on her face made me smile.

One person who did not smile was Mack on the day the Red Sox picked him. He had rooted for the big-league Yankees for years, even before my YES job came about. He would study the Yankees' history: Ruth, Gehrig, Berra, DiMaggio, Mantle, Jackson, Mattingly, Jeter, Rivera, and the big moments they'd all delivered. He held no desire to sport enemy garb, and I'm sure it wouldn't have pleased Steinbrenner either. The boy wanted an interlocking "N-Y" on his cap.

So I arranged the greatest trade in Scarsdale baseball history, at least according to me. I somehow found the father of a Little League Yankees player who wished to join the Red Sox. Over a pair of ice cream cones, the father and I talked things over. We agreed to give each boy what he wanted.

My son was a Yankee. Time to treat him like one.

I TOOK Mack where the New York Yankees train each spring. Today it's known as George M. Steinbrenner Field, the largest spring training ballpark in Florida, with a life-sized bronze statue of the eponym watching over the entrance. But back then it was called Legends Field, which didn't need a statue because the real-life Steinbrenner stood in the flesh. On our way down onto the playing surface, when elevator doors opened, we saw him.

Steinbrenner turned his neck and smiled once the doors closed. It had been a while since I'd seen him look anything but gruff.

He bended his knees and extended his arm. "Well, who is this?"

"This is my son, Mack," I told him. "Mack, meet Mr. Steinbrenner."

"How are you, Mack?" Steinbrenner asked. "Having fun?"

"Yes, I am, sir."

"You see that, Fred? He says *sir*!"

Steinbrenner raised his chin and nodded in the affirmative. He had just chewed out some prospects for coming to camp with beards, which violated the club's personal grooming policy, but he had nothing to worry about with ten-year-old Mack. "And your son doesn't have any facial hair. That's a *real* team player!"

The elevator door opened. He asked one last question before we took the field. "Is Mack left-handed?"

"In fact, he is," I said.

He winked. "Good to know."

Legends awaited us. I told Mack to stay in the dugout and soak it all in while I taped interviews for YES. One of my favorite chats was with Yogi Berra, one of the best catchers who ever lived, whose ten World Series rings and infinite wordplay will never be beaten. Lines such as "It ain't over 'til it's over," "You can observe a lot by watching," and "The future ain't what it used to be" capture his genius.

Yogi spotted me near home plate. "Hey, I know you," he said. "You do the show before the show and the show after the show."

"You caught me red-handed!" I told him. "Thank you so much for watching."

"Do you like it here?" he asked.

I mentioned how glad I was to see all these greats, including him, in person. "I'm usually at the studio in Connecticut."

"Wow, Connecticut! That's far. Well, I'll tell you what. You're doing well here over there."

After thanking Yogi—and spending minutes trying to make sense of his syntax—I looked toward the dugout. Mack had just handed shortstop Derek Jeter my cell phone. Derek, the soon-to-be-named captain, was using the phone to say hi to one of my son's classmates.

Seconds after Derek hung up, the same phone rang. I hustled over and answered it. It was the classmate's father.

"Fred, I'm so sorry to bother you," the father said. "But my son must be lying. He just bragged and said he spoke with Jeter. This can't be true, can it?"

I told the dad that his kid wasn't lying. Like Yogi, Derek was just that kind of role model, always lifting spirits, and ever mindful that crowds of all ages looked up to him. In a word: integrity.

Another titan of the game, Yankees manager Joe Torre, walked over minutes later. He and I had first met two decades earlier, during his time as the Atlanta Braves' skipper. He had since managed the Yanks to four World Series crowns. His voice, his forward-leaning shuffle, and the calm in his eyes defined gravitas under pressure.

I jokingly asked Joe, "Which position do you want me to play?"

FAST FORWARD TO NOVEMBER 2003—AND me wearing Yankee pinstripes. No, this wasn't the World Series, which New York had recently lost to the Florida Marlins. This was New York Yankees fantasy camp, a weeklong chance for lifelong fans to suit up and play against their favorite retired players. Doctors, lawyers, and CEOs had shelled out thousands to partake. As a team broadcaster, I got in free.

I stank. Before an exhibition between the Campers and the Old-Timers, my fellow Campers took one look at my practice swing and demanded a trade. So the Old-Timers, which included Yankee greats Willie Randolph and Ron Guidry, made the mistake of bringing me onboard.

More blunders ensued. After legendary public-address announcer Bob Sheppard introduced me—*"Now batting: Fred Hickman"*—I swung and missed on three straight pitches nowhere near the strike zone. Then while I was playing shortstop, a fly ball dropped right in front of me.

Willie, playing his usual second base, couldn't stop laughing. "Dude, are your cleats stuck? You've got to actually *move* to get the ball!"

I couldn't help but laugh with him. The Campers enjoyed it too, having gotten their money's worth by trading me when they did. And for me, getting to taste Guidry's homemade Louisiana gumbo that week was worth all the dropped balls on Earth.

As if playing a full baseball game for the first time in decades didn't make me feel rusty enough, I reprised another long-lost role. Only this time, I had the most honest critics of all to impress: children.

I went to the White House to do play-by-play for a kids' T-ball game. As odd as that sentence may seem now, youth sporting events on the mansion's South Lawn were frequent during George W. Bush's presidency. The commander-in-chief, formerly a part-owner and top hypeman for baseball's Texas Rangers, loved the chance to trade his suit for a polo and slacks—and cheer in the bleachers like the good ol' days.

There was also a greater purpose to this particular game. Its players—from Glen Burnie, Maryland, and Ridley Park, Pennsylvania—had various intellectual and physical disabilities. Its date coincided with the anniversary of the Americans with Disabilities Act, which the first President Bush had signed in 1990. In between my announcing each name and calling each play, parents cried happy tears. I felt a lump in my throat myself, especially after players in walkers and wheelchairs rushed to home plate to celebrate a teammate's home run. That's dedication.

We didn't keep score. Being there marked a victory in itself for these kids. And if anything, not keeping score made announcing easier for me, as I hadn't done play-by-play since Atlanta Hawks basketball in 1981. I was just glad I didn't botch any names.

We all gathered for a picnic afterward. Hot dogs and burgers. I asked the president why he'd picked me, of all broadcasters, to sit behind the microphone.

He opened his arms. "We're baseball guys!"

No argument there. We spent a few minutes rattling off old trivia, rosters of yore, and grade-school memories of sneaking transistors into class to hear the World Series. Whatever your politics, his appreciation of the sport as a cultural bridge runs deep.

Two years later, President Bush invited me onto his lawn again. This time, it was to call a Little League T-ball game between the Black Yankees of Newark, New Jersey, and the Memphis Red Sox of Chicago. That's right: two majority-Black youth teams, from low-income neighborhoods, named after Negro League clubs from the early 1900s. Though most original Black Yankees and Memphis Red Sox players were no longer alive, at least their team names were. The names' presence that day outside our democratic republic's highest-profile residence felt like a national embrace of long-underappreciated players—a homecoming.

But circumstances at my own home were turning less festive. I was now my family's lone breadwinner. I left YES for a job that was farther away but involved more money. I would soon learn the cost.

With Judy and Mack.

11

OF BRISTOL
AND BATTLES

THE TALLEST BUILDING IN BRISTOL HAS NO WINDOWS. It's the Otis Elevator Test Tower. Elevators go up—high above maples, oaks, birches, and beeches—and elevators go down. Life in the bucolic central Connecticut valley town, which in the nineteenth century had been a clockmaking capital, now ticked more slowly.

Except at the Entertainment and Sports Programming Network's headquarters. By the time I became a *SportsCenter* anchor in December 2004, the channel's 116-acre campus had evolved into the so-nicknamed "Mothership." Beyond the editing booths, glass-encased studios, and thirty-one-dish satellite farm, the place boasted motion sensors, gourmet cuisine, rooftop seating, a basketball court, a Starbucks, a duck pond, foosball tables, a gym, group workouts, and a staff of thousands. Two central emergency generator facilities, aptly named Central Emergency Generator Facility 1 and 2, could power the compound for days after external grid failures. And as Bristol's largest taxpayer, ESPN kept the paved roads smooth.

But for all the whistles and amenities, nothing could replace family.

. . .

JUDY WAS GETTING WORSE. Her multiple sclerosis now left her unable to walk. She could barely talk. She didn't leave the house, except for doctor's appointments or hospital stays. No parent-teacher conferences. No Little League games. No recitals. And because her illness's complications had already done enough to separate her from Mack and Gabby, she told me, "No nursing home." All she asked was to sleep under the same roof as our children.

We had discussed moving closer to Bristol, but her growing frailty made an eighty-mile move feel impossible. Besides, the kids were already going through such scary times with her. We decided that changing schools wouldn't have helped. They needed stability. They needed to stay in Scarsdale. If that meant me driving up to four hours a day either to or from a job that funded our mounting medical bills, I was willing to do it.

But we did make some adjustments. I hired an at-home nurse. I booked house calls for physical therapists. I got a nanny for the kids. I found a maid to keep our place as clean for an immunocompromised person as could be. I bought a hospital bed—with rails and all—and set it up in our spare bedroom, next to a list of all our doctors' and pharmacies' phone numbers.

The setup worked at first. Mack and Gabby would return from school and recount their daily adventures with such crisp detail, Judy often said it felt like she had been with them all day. Though the West Coast *SportsCenters* often kept me from getting home before four a.m., I'd usually pop my head into her room whenever I arrived, to make sure she was okay. Sometimes she would already be awake and lying there in the dark, so we'd pray for the strength to keep going. And nobody could tell us visiting hours were over.

Yet as months passed, a chain of complications made me lose count. Infections. Injuries. Phone calls during work. Cries awakening me, telling me Judy needed an emergency room. Hospital stays. Close calls.

Each time I checked her out of the hospital, I would lug home whatever new gadget the doctors had recommended. I didn't know if insurance would cover it. I just knew it was heavy and loud —and that it would buy us at least a little more time.

FOR YEARS, even after Judy's diagnosis, I had considered myself the human Energizer bunny. I tended to her and the kids. I worked. I cooked, did laundry, grocery shopped, picked up prescriptions, shuttled the kids around, and made sure homework was done. I had gone years, maybe a decade, without so much as a cold. But even the best batteries need replacing.

Exhaustion overcame me. Less than a year into my ESPN job, my nightly average of just four hours of sleep caught up with my body. My chest would tighten for hours on end. The mere act of walking down a hallway, or even driving around a curve, would leave me winded. I gained weight despite not having time to eat.

But I refused to stop. Whatever my struggle, Judy had it worse. My kids also had it worse than I did; I worried they would soon be without a living mother. They all relied on me to pay the bills, stay strong, and never give up.

Easier said than done. My job performance began to slip. I began to show up late. I didn't have the energy to come to campus early and tape "This is *SportsCenter*" commercials the way my colleagues did. I fell behind on writing scripts. I stumbled during anchor reads. I would rush to a cafeteria, bathroom, or hallway to take long phone calls from my wife's doctors, then I would barely get onto the set by airtime. Each time someone asked if everything was okay, I'd dismiss them with an out-of-breath "I'm sorry about that."

I could see on my colleagues' faces that my actions had irked them, but I felt it wasn't my place to use Judy's illness as an excuse. Her privacy was not mine to breach. And ESPN wasn't exactly paying me all this money to complain. So I kept my mouth shut.

Until one night on Interstate 84.

I MUST HAVE DRIVEN for twenty miles before realizing I was driving at all. The clock blinked "3:05 a.m." The speedometer measured sixty-six miles an hour. Signs indicated I was near Middlebury. Yet I couldn't recall leaving Bristol. Not good.

I pulled onto the shoulder and wept. Years of tears geysered out of me. I stayed there for about twenty minutes, convulsing inside my car, thinking of how I could've veered off the road by driving under such a mental haze. I could've killed myself. I could've killed someone else. All my efforts to provide for my family would've been for nought. I couldn't let that happen.

I took a few deep breaths, turned some music on, slapped my cheeks dry, and drove an hour to White Plains Hospital. At this point, Judy was spending more time there than at our home. I planned to pop in with some family photos for her bedside.

A doctor spotted me in the hallway the moment I arrived. "Why are you here?"

"What do you mean?" I asked back.

"Most people I know in your position don't do all you've done to keep her going."

"The thought of anything else never crossed my mind."

I meant what I'd told him, but Judy and I did have to decide our future. She was becoming more bedridden by the day. Her organs were taking turns attacking her. It was clear from this hospital stay that our house, despite the nurses and equipment, could no longer meet her needs. We had to consider a nursing home.

That morning, I called a friend who happened to be a New

York doctor. He was one of the few people who knew about Judy's condition. I told him, "I really don't know what to do."

"Let me stop you there," he said. "The only choice now is that you don't have a choice. You have to do this. Who's going to take care of you? Who's going to take care of your kids?"

The doctor placed one hand on my shoulder. He pointed the other at me.

WITH JUDY'S BLESSING, I finally told my bosses what was going on. They agreed to stay mum. They said, "Take all the time you need," so I did. I was blessed to have a workplace like ESPN in my corner.

I was also thankful for Harold Reynolds. The *Baseball Tonight* analyst, whom I had known since his playing days, was one of the few other work people I'd told. Instead of saying "If there's anything I can do . . ." without follow-through, he took action. He told me he was building a house for himself and wanted to sell his old condominium in West Hartford. The condo was just fifteen minutes from the ESPN campus and less than ten from a great nursing home. He offered me a next-to-nothing deal. A true friend.

But I couldn't take Harold's offer without first getting Judy into that nearby facility. A few tours and many phone calls later, I determined that it was the place for her. The staffers were friendly and knew their stuff. The building sat within a few miles of more than one hospital. And by moving all of us to central Connecticut, I could finally spend less time driving (or sobbing) and more time hugging my family.

There was, however, a catch. The nursing home risked costing more than $100,000 a year, even with our joint health insurance policy. Though we would free up money by selling the Scarsdale house, downsizing into the condo, and no longer needing visiting nurses, the price was still hefty, especially after having spent roughly $1 million for at-home help and equipment. Sure, I'd pay whatever was required, but I at least had to seek a less costly way to get her in.

I called an attorney who suggested divorce. He said ending our marriage, legally speaking, would allow Judy to qualify for Medicaid. Instead of us paying a fortune out of pocket, Uncle Sam would cover her care. And we'd still have enough assets to pass down to our kids someday.

The financial upside didn't change how wrong the advice felt. A decade and a half earlier, Judy and I had said, "In sickness and in health . . . I do." If someone had told me then that obtaining affordable health care would require ending a marriage, especially in a superpower like the United States of America, I never would've believed it. Yet such was our pre-Obamacare dilemma.

After many nights of prayer, we signed off on a divorce. It was the toughest decision we ever made, but we both knew our shared truth. We still loved one another. We were still devoted, more now than ever, to the family we had built. And thanks to the understanding staff at her new nursing home, I could still be by her side.

When I wasn't working or sleeping, I was with Judy. I would visit two or three times a day. Sometimes the kids would join me. Other times, friends I hardly knew I had were already there to help.

Jackie was one of those people. I had met her through Harold, and soon she felt like family in her own right. She kept Judy company when I couldn't be at the nursing home. She watched the kids while I worked. And when I told her how exhausted I still felt, even after relocating closer to work, she urged stubborn old me to see a doctor.

Good timing. Had I not listened to Jackie, I never would've asked relatives about my family's medical history. I never would've learned about the heart defect that had accelerated my father's death. Nor would my own heart have received the help it apparently needed.

But as new medication and different work hours raised my stamina, Judy was reaching the point of no return. She could no longer eat nor breathe on her own. It was, as a doctor at one hospital said, "a matter of when."

After a particularly rough night, Jackie recommended that I do something for myself.

"Like what?" I asked her.

"Whatever feels right," she said.

So I kissed Judy, returned to my condo, and took a late-winter stroll—just me and my Sony Walkman. Halfway down the block, I paused the music. All I heard now were wind gusts and footsteps. I looked around. I was five minutes from home but couldn't recognize a thing. The yards, trees, neighbors, and dogs were all new to me. Even after more than a year in West Hartford, I guess I had been too busy to acquaint myself.

I retraced the wet footprints that my boots had left on the sidewalk. I hit my Walkman's play button again and found my way back. Just in time for my phone to ring.

JUDY DIED ON A MONDAY. A coworker called me that Tuesday.

"Fred, I'm so sorry."

"Thank you."

"No, really. I am sorry."

The colleague told me she hadn't realized the extent of my family's struggle. She said she would have been kinder to me had she known. I hadn't thought of her as unkind, but I appreciated her sentiment.

"Knowing you," she added, "you did everything you could for Judy."

The kind words lifted a weight. I didn't think so much about what I could have done differently. Instead came gratitude for the kindness people can show when they know the facts.

As my children and I shed tears, the thought of Judy no longer in pain brought at least some comfort. Her peace began nurturing mine. Even if my instincts were telling me to leave ESPN. Even if I didn't know what to do next.

12

NICK'S LAST FIGHT

"If ever you're afraid," said the man who had coanchored with me longer than anyone, "think of a boxer."

Boxers confront fear. They play the loneliest sport. The lights of the room burn on them. Their skin and blood are exposed. One move can cripple them. Nobody else can punch or block for them in the ring. But if great people stand in their corner, cleaning them up after each round, they can hold on a bit longer.

If you ask me, Nick Charles was a boxer.

Nick got bladder cancer. He was diagnosed in 2009, by which point it had already reached his lungs. He took leave from his job at Showtime, where he'd been a boxing commentator since exiting CNN in 2001. Dark crescents formed under his eyes. Chemotherapy stole his famous hair—but not his mind.

I called whenever possible. More than once, after I dialed Nick's room at Houston's MD Anderson Cancer Center, a floor nurse answered. "Mr. Charles isn't available," she said each time. "He's in the hallway doing pushups."

He exercised not for vanity but for necessity. There were still

88

things in life he needed to do. Cook osso buco. Record birthday videos for young daughter Giovanna and wife Cory to watch years later. Hear Giovanna play piano. Reread his favorite world classics. See the opera again. Build a dream house in New Mexico that overlooked the Sangre de Cristo Mountains. Announce play-by-play for one last televised boxing fight.

Sports Illustrated got word of the diagnosis. One of the magazine's writers, Joe Posnanski, met Nick in Santa Fe. They spent an afternoon together for an interview. They walked downtown. They talked about sunsets. They paused at times to notice a Spanish cemetery or catch a breath. A winded Nick conceded that his wish to call a final boxing match probably wouldn't come true. "It's okay," he told Joe. "I've covered a lot of fights."

But word spread. The interview made *Sports Illustrated's* March 7, 2011, issue. A loyal reader named Rick Bernstein read a copy during a morning train ride to his job—as executive producer for HBO's boxing telecasts. And it gave Rick an idea.

On the night of March 26, Nick got his fight. He stood under the lights of Atlantic City's Boardwalk Hall, HBO microphone in hand, and called a *Boxing After Dark* showdown between undefeated featherweights Matt Remillard and Mikey Garcia. "Why am I doing this tonight?" he said. "To inspire others to do what you love."

After ten rounds, Remillard surrendered. But Nick, despite being prepared and strong enough to have gone all twelve, didn't curse the sudden end. In the broadcast's closing minutes, he concluded his forty-year career with a thank you.

The world, however, wasn't done thanking him.

Nick took a few hours away from his pushups, cooking, and housebuilding to see me one last time. He had lost weight, and I had gained it. I guess we always balanced each other out.

We reminisced about it all. The high school basketball games in

Springfield. The Slim Whitman album. The clunky typewriters at CNN with Nick's name all over them. The Ford Tempo we'd driven into the limo line at the awards banquet. All the bugs who'd bit us in Russia. The voodoo priestess we'd met in New Orleans. Nick's exotic trips to the Himalayas or anywhere else with pack animals and sherpas. That time we put staples in our ears because some expert thought it would help us quit cigarettes. So many Super Bowls, Fall Classics, and "Plays of the Day." Grand-marshaling the 1996 Illinois State Fair Parade together. Our joy in fatherhood. His excitement seeing the 2005 Chicago White Sox winning the World Series, the team's first since 1917. (If only he could've seen my face after my Cubs broke their own championship drought in 2016, following 108 long years.)

Nick would receive piles of letters. Their messages included "KEEP FIGHTING" and "DON'T STOP PUNCHING." Our younger wordsmithing selves probably would've dismissed them as cheesy, trite, or saccharine, but life had given Nick the courage to stop caring about that. "There's no time to give a damn about whether this or that sounds corny," he said. "Just hold onto it all."

To him, even the time between diagnosis and death was a gift. "I've had twenty months that people are validating my life," he would tell *The Baltimore Sun* in his final weeks. "If I had gotten run over by a bus, it would have been a nice eulogy, but I never would have heard it."

I can only pray to live my dying days as graciously and gracefully as Nick lived his.

We hugged.

"Thank you," I told him. "For everything."

The former Chicago cabbie—who had spent childhood nights shivering under covers, who'd been told early in his TV career that his Greek features made him look too ethnic, who'd befriended and helped a young Black man from Springfield beat addiction—

didn't skip a beat. "I guess we scrappy boys from Illinois did okay after all."

One of the last things he did was finish his mountainside dream house. He helped movers place a piano in his living room. He walked into Giovanna's closet and smiled thinking about the prom dress she would someday hang in there. He used one word to describe the new view from his window: "Heaven."

His final words to me were "I'll see you later."

With Braves player-turned-broadcaster Brian Jordan (center) and Chicago Cubs legend Ernie Banks (right), a childhood favorite of this Illinois boy's.

With Ron Gant (center), another former Brave who became a broadcast partner, and special guest Hank Aaron (right), the man behind 755 career home runs.

Covering Saints football for WVUE in New Orleans. Also pictured: broadcaster Dave Sims (left) and Hall of Fame wide receiver James Lofton (right).

13

NEW TRICKS

The year Nick died, I ate my fifty-fifth birthday cake in slower bites. Not only was my pal gone, but the first TV news director who had ever hired me—the coincidentally named Don Hickman—would die later that year. And I was only a year from my father's age of death. More than ever, I grasped what the best athletes had told me throughout my career: Life's deepest revelations bloom from loss.

That's when I decided how to spend my remaining years. Not burning out. Not chasing jobs that would've stripped me of fatherly time. Not pigeonholing myself. I instead wanted a way to spread my late mentors' lessons while learning new tricks of my own. I was ready to see what else this old dog could do.

And I knew who I wanted by my side.

I had met Sheila a few years earlier, at a mutual friend's dinner party in Connecticut. It had taken me almost an hour to find the restaurant on my glitchy GPS screen. Given all I had been through with Judy, it felt like years since I'd socialized. But after seeing and talking to Sheila for the first time, I knew she was worth the effort and more. Gone were the fears that I had lost all social skills. Troubles melted. Food tasted better. Narrow roads looked wider.

We've been each other's cheerleaders ever since. Through every risk and reward.

WE MARRIED and took chances down south. I was back in Atlanta, this time working as a studio host for Braves baseball on Fox Sports South. Many of the channel's behind-the-scenes rascals had worked at CNN Sports before CNN/SI's fall, and returning to the city made for fun recollections. We would all laugh about the Braves' bad old days of the late 1970s and most of the 1980s, how Ted Turner had begged us to fill stadium seats, and how the team had grown to dominate in the '90s.

The job was freelance, which left room for a passion project. I decided to give media coaching a try, hoping to help sports figures avoid the proverbial communication dumpster fires. For decades, I had seen even the most gifted players and team coaches either freeze on camera, say the wrong thing, avoid eye contact, or shoo reporters away; I'd also seen too many retired athletes crumble because they thought their best years were behind them. Being in the early days of smartphones, I was saddened to see up-and-comers taint their hopes because they didn't know social media rants were considered on-the-record remarks. So by meeting clients wherever they were—home, the locker room, the weight room, in a different city—a side hustle called Fred Hickman Communications took flight.

My most prized pupils grew to approach media training like fitness training. They tackled each day with discipline and appreciated the process. On loop and in slow motion, they spent time reviewing the mock pregame and postgame interviews we had taped together. When they faced a camera lens, they envisioned speaking to one specific person instead of the whole world at once. Instead of getting lost in the internet's cesspools of bad-faith criticism, they sought out constructive input from people who actually knew what they were talking about. By the time our lessons were done, they were smiling more, looking at interviewers' eyes more, and taking more time to serve others.

Sure, I gave the advice, but my clients are the ones who have changed communities with it. One has become a beloved face in a big city. Another has used his public speaking skills to raise funds for charities. Another, a retired player, has found new life in broadcasting. I won't namedrop, but you may have seen some of these folks on your TV.

Which brings me back to my own on-air career. In 2011 and with support from the misses, I became sports director at WVUE, the Fox affiliate in New Orleans. The city promised heavy helpings of jambalaya, gumbo, summer rain, and juicy sports stories; and it did not disappoint. Louisiana State University's first-ranked football Tigers played one of their strongest seasons ever, not counting the 21-0 shutout to Alabama in the championship game. Saints football owner Tom Benson's purchase of what would become the Pelicans ensured that bounce music's birthplace was in the National Basketball Association to stay. And of course, the Bountygate scandal—in which the Saints clubhouse slipped non-contract bonuses to defensive players who knocked targeted opponents out of games—led the National Football League to deliver its first-ever suspensions of a head coach and a general manager. These were newsworthy times, yet even with this full-time job, I still found a few hours a week to do media coaching for former athletes in need.

If New Orleans taught me anything, it was that Louisiana folks love their high school sports. Bumper stickers are one thing, but I had never before lived in a state where drivers could get license plates customized with a varsity logo. I learned quickly that when Louisianians ask "Where'd ya go to school?" they mean high school, and that only outsiders give universities as answers. Lest we forget that nothing, and I mean nothing, drives community spirit there like Friday night lights. To me, these all resembled signs of a state that valued its next generation. I respected that.

And unbeknownst to me, an adventure was brewing that would pair me with the next generation of broadcast journalists.

IT WAS a phone call I had never expected. From a smaller city. About a job I'd never imagined having. Yet the more I heard, the cooler this opportunity seemed.

The caller was Gary Wordlaw, a television lifer known to bust barriers. He had gone from sweeping floors in the 1960s, as a Chattanooga station's first Black employee, to leading newsrooms in Seattle, Baltimore, and D.C. and teaching journalism at Syracuse University. He had retired once or twice but couldn't kick the broadcasting bug. Now in his mid-sixties, he was plotting one of his most daring leaps yet, revamping WVLA-TV, the third-place NBC affiliate in Baton Rouge, Louisiana.

"I want you as a senior member of my staff," he told me.

"Evening sports anchor?" I asked.

"Evening *news* anchor."

That's right. Not sports but news. How's that for a gamble?

"Is it that crazy an idea?" he asked.

"Only one way to find out!"

I know many sports guys who dream of transitioning to news, but few people believe them. Bosses laugh and tell them, "You're a jock. News ain't for you." What those bosses don't say is that sports-reporting experience is a strength in newsrooms, not a novelty. A good sports broadcaster can improvise more quickly and show the different sides at stake more clearly, whatever the story. As for me, it was refreshing that a man of faith like Gary saw what others didn't.

I took the job. It didn't take long to see that for what was then the nation's ninety-third-largest TV market, Baton Rouge produces a lot of headlines. The city has held one of America's highest crime rates. As a state capital, the home of one of the nation's largest oil refineries is also where policymakers discuss

Louisiana's record-fast coastal land loss. And at 450 feet, its legislative tower stands taller than any other in the country, with the political folklore to match.

I had reported on heavyweight fights before but none as surreal as the 2015 Louisiana governor's race. To quote the campaign ad that eventually wound up on Comedy Central's *The Daily Show*, the duel was between "[Democrat] John Bel Edwards, who answered our country's call and served as a Ranger in the 82nd Airborne Division . . . or [Republican Senator] David Vitter, who answered a prostitute's call." *Ouch.* Vitter's phone number had indeed appeared in call logs from the so-called "D.C. Madam" some sixteen years earlier. Vitter had also spied on a primary rival by hiring a private investigator who later got caught hiding behind an air-conditioning unit. (Yet somehow, this gubernatorial matchup was not the state's wackiest ever, as the 1991 race had ended with future federal inmate Edwin Edwards beating former Ku Klux Klan grand wizard David Duke.)

Moderating the final debate between John Bel Edwards and David Vitter made Super Bowls seem quiet and tackle-free. I began by telling the four hundred spectators behind me to hold their reactions until the end, though in a high school auditorium out for blood, my request did next to nothing. The partisan audience divided themselves between cheers, boos, chants, and heckles. The contenders, amped up by the noise, used every chance to call the other a hypocrite, which only stirred the masses further.

More than once, I unleashed my inner referee. I limited rebuttals to fifteen seconds and told the candidates to move on too many times to count. "I would like to ask the audience to please hold your applause," I said at one point, "because we have an awful lot to get to."

Edwards gave me one look. "I don't think that's going to work, Fred," he said, as if toweling off before a new round. And for the rest of the night, before a crowd that was close and loud enough to sound like forty thousand people, he laid out his opponent.

The guy landed burn after burn. After Vitter cited Edwards's failing grade from a business lobbyist group, Edwards said, "I give 100 percent to my wife. . . . Senator, you ought to try." After Vitter criticized Edwards's "interesting" use of a party bus for a get-out-the-vote event, Edwards replied, "Not as interesting as your date night, senator!" Vitter admitted he was wrong and requested forgiveness, to which Edwards fired back, "We're all obliged as Christians to forgive, but that doesn't have to mean we forget." Edwards, a Democrat once dismissed as ruby-red Louisiana's long-shot contender, sealed a victory that would become official five nights later.

What a fiery bout. Minutes after my adventure in debate-moderating ended, I approached a floor crew member who knew a thing or two about boxing refs. I looked at him, took a giant swig of water, and said, "God bless Mills Lane."

But that November clash was tame compared to the heat that summer would bring.

I WATCHED the forty-eight-second video at my desk with my hands on my temples. Recorded on a phone and sent to the newsroom early on July 5, 2016, it showed Baton Rouge police pinning a Black man who had been selling CDs outside a convenience store. Officers knelt over the man's chest and thigh in the parking lot. Moments after one officer shouted, "He's got a gun!" the other fired six shots. By the end, the man they had pinned was lifeless on his back, his already-red shirt stained a darker shade, his hands empty, his handgun untouched in his right pocket.

The footage circulated fast. My colleagues and I were still making calls, looking into what had prompted the gunfire, and planning to cover nights of protests, but this much we already knew: The world was about to learn Alton Sterling's name.

We spent that night all over the city. Nonviolent demonstrators filled intersections. Strangers from near and far placed flowers and candles at the shooting site. Fireworks unused during America's 240th birthday were lit to denounce racism within the nation's institutions.

And the week wasn't over. I awoke that Thursday to learn that police had shot and killed another Black man. This time, it was during a traffic stop in Falcon Heights, Minnesota. The deceased was a school cafeteria supervisor named Philando Castile, pulled over because of a broken taillight. This killing, about 1,200 miles from the scene of Sterling's death, was enough for one Baton Rouge protester to tell me, "Déjà vu."

That night in Dallas, during what had been a peaceful Black Lives Matter demonstration, a Black gunman seeking revenge shot twelve police officers, killing five.

Concerns grew that a copycat ambush would happen in Baton Rouge, specifically because that's where Sterling had lived and died. Shortly after the Dallas shooting, an FBI warning referenced a social media user's plot to "purge" Louisiana cops. Police subsequently confiscated three rifles, three shotguns, and two pistols after uncovering a plan to shoot officers during that weekend's protests. At one demonstration, a protester knocked a BRPD officer's teeth out with a rock. And as local journalists, we got angry mail just for reporting on these tensions: "Nobody would be hurting and killing police if y'all didn't inflate BLM"; "You better hope no more cops are slaughtered, for your own sake." Those viewers had no clue that before bed each night since July 5, I had been praying that every officer and civilian return home safe.

Attending and covering Sterling's funeral left me hopeful. Before thousands of mourners at Southern University on July 15, Reverend Jesse Jackson said, "We must choose reconciliation over retaliation and revenge." Reverend Al Sharpton reminded the crowd that Baton Rouge was where the first civil rights bus boycott had caught Martin Luther King's attention in 1953. "This is the birthplace, where it started," Sharpton said, "and this is the birthplace we come back to today." Convenience store owner

Abdullah Muflahi closed his eulogy by quoting Dr. King: "Hate cannot drive out hate. Only love can do that." The choir closed with "Ain't No Need to Worry," a Winans Family song about how nights don't last and how morning will come.

Two mornings later, the poignant lyric about eternal peace met a haunting contrast.

I GOT a call that Sunday morning. I was still in church clothes. A voice asked from the other end. "How soon can you get to the newsroom?"

A short drive later, colleague Lauren McCoy and I interrupted programming to deliver breaking news: Someone had shot six local law enforcement officers near a gas station on Airline Highway. Three of the officers were dead; a fourth had injuries that years later proved fatal. Sirens and flashing lights filled what was usually one of Baton Rouge's busiest stretches. Ambulances rushed the surviving officers to nearby hospitals. The shooter, whom we later learned was an avowed Black separatist, was killed by a responding SWAT officer less than ten minutes after the ambush. And the city I had grown to love, already hurting, was again in focus.

We learned the fallen officers' names. Brad Garafola had spent almost a quarter-century with the East Baton Rouge Parish Sheriff's Office. Nick Tullier, who would die in May 2022, had served as a sergeant with the sheriff's office. Matthew Gerald had served in the Marines before joining the BRPD. Montrell Jackson, a ten-year BRPD veteran of color, had posted on Facebook days before the shooting that claimed his life:

> Please don't let hate infect your heart. This city MUST and WILL get better. I'm working in these streets so any protesters, officers, friends, family, or whoever, if you see me and need a hug or want to say a prayer, I got you.

Jackson's words stuck with me through each officer's funerals. They still do.

Life is too short not to extend a hand.

SHAQUILLE O'NEAL WAS MORE upset than I had thought. It was early 2017, more than half a year after Golden State Warriors point guard Stephen Curry had become the NBA's first unanimously elected Most Valuable Player. Shaq, at this point a studio analyst on *Inside the NBA*, called me out on national TV. "I would've been the first unanimous MVP, and some guy from Atlanta, Fred Dumb Hickman—" he said before fellow legend Charles Barkley tried talking him down, to no avail.

"If I see Fred Hickman in the street, there are gonna be some stop signs moving," Shaq continued. "You messed up history, Fred."

Listen. For me, covering the violence of 2016 had put the world into perspective. I didn't regret picking Allen Iverson on my 2000 MVP ballot, but I did regret that almost seventeen years had passed without me making amends with the big man. It was time to build a bridge.

I delivered my message on WVLA's Friday night sports show:

> I love you, Shaq. . . . I proudly display one of your shoes in my home. Speaking of home, by the way, that's what Baton Rouge is for me now. We do know that you love LSU and Baton Rouge. The next time you're in town, Big Aristotle, we'll break the bread. We'll make the peace. My treat. Cost is no object. You're a Hall of Famer. You're one of the all-time greats.

Shaq and I finally met up that February, during the NBA All-Star Weekend in New Orleans. As I walked toward him inside the Smoothie King Center, he saw me across the room and gave a playful smirk. A handshake became an embrace. No punches. No rehashing of words said long ago. No denying or dismissing each other's feelings. Only respect.

We took a photo for doubters who wanted proof. That was our treaty.

Even if society can't mend all divisions that easily, I left that day a grateful man. I hope Shaq did too.

An afternoon with Shaq.

With Sheila.

With coanchor Jeanne Burns (front, center-right) and much of the cast and crew at WVLA-TV in Baton Rouge.

Serving the D.C. market on WDVM-TV, with coanchor Tasmin Mahfuz.

Reenacting a monologue from the 1972 film The Godfather, *a classic.*

14

PASSING THE TORCH

In case you cannot tell, I am Black. I always have been. On occasion, society has reminded me of this fact.

The racial tensions of 2016 helped me see, or at least reminded me of, what hadn't changed since my youth. Black kids still struggled to find toys and picture books that reflected their skin tones. Black teens and adults still faced claims of being too stoic, too emotional, too lazy, or too ambitious, sometimes all at once. News directors at certain TV stations were still snubbing non-White job candidates because they thought viewers, even after all this time, weren't "ready." Certain White people still thought they were complimenting Black people by telling them, "You don't sound Black." At certain schools, Black students were being sent home for wearing dreadlocks or braids. It was never more clear that the presidential election eight years earlier of Barack Obama, who had announced his candidacy on the Old State Capitol steps in my hometown of Springfield, Illinois, had not ended racism. Prejudice still filled a spectrum as broad as race itself.

And two years later, athletes who followed the decades-old paths of Bill Russell, Muhammad Ali, Tommie Smith, Roberto

Clemente, Curt Flood, and others by denouncing injustice were told to "shut up and dribble."

My anger turned into sadness. On a lazy weekend afternoon, I walked to the bookcase in my home office. Staring back at me were pages upon pages on slavery, Reconstruction, Black Wall Street, the Tuskegee Airmen, and the civil rights movement of the 1950s and '60s. In full detail were the courageous deeds of Dr. King, John Lewis, Rosa Parks, Thurgood Marshall, Medgar Evers, and their contemporaries. Yet even with enough books to bury me if they were to fall all at once, I couldn't help but think of all that was missing: histories that hadn't been made, dreams unrealized.

I left the house and found stories worth telling. One was that of Cornelius Hawkins, one of 272 people sold to Louisiana plantation owners to fund Georgetown University's 1838 expansion. With his great-granddaughter, I walked around the cane fields of Maringouin, Louisiana—just twenty-five miles west of Baton Rouge—where Mr. Hawkins and many of the other enslaved people had been buried. I met Georgetown president John DeGioia, who decided to right the university's wrong by offering priority admission to descendants of the enslaved. Though a small step, the move showed how being honest about the past and present can better the future.

Speaking of the future, the man I called "boss" started concocting his next big project.

"WE'RE CALLING it the Black News Channel," Gary Wordlaw told me in 2019. "It'll be nationally available on cable, by Black people, for Black people. I want you as my lead anchor."

He was onto something. For all the hyper-specialized cable news and opinion mills on television, none portrayed Black communities with much depth. Despite a survey showing them watching more TV than any other U.S. group and totaling at least $1.3 trillion in buying power, Black Americans had made up less than 12 percent of the nation's TV news staffs in 2018, according to the Radio Television Digital News Association; only 2 percent of American TV news directors were Black. No wonder news programs were barely addressing topics such as sickle cell disease, historically Black colleges and universities, or non-urban Black populations.

We had a gap to fill.

I told Gary, who would serve as BNC's vice president for news, "Let's get to work."

It seemed early on that BNC would deliver on its mission. Its founding chairman, former Republican congressman J. C. Watts, welcomed voices with diverse backgrounds and views. Shows such as *D.C. Today*, *Being a Woman*, *Today's Teen*, and my nightly newscast each aimed to unpack the many layers of the Black experience. Beyond having correspondents in Atlanta, Chicago, Los Angeles, New York, and Philadelphia, the channel built its headquarters near Florida A&M University, an HBCU in Tallahassee. Students and aspiring journalists had a pipeline to hone their craft. Experienced storytellers had somewhere to share ancestral wisdom.

But not long after Sheila and I unpacked our bags and boxes, we endured challenges of our own. We all did.

BNC LAUNCHED IN FEBRUARY 2020. To paraphrase a fellow author: It was the best of timing, it was the worst of timing.

Let's start with the worst. The year had begun with a plane crash that killed Los Angeles Lakers icon Kobe Bryant, who had matured into a caring mentor for so many athletes. The racially motivated murder of Ahmaud Arbery that February in Georgia, the police killing of Breonna Taylor that March in Kentucky, and the murder of George Floyd by a White police officer in Minnesota that May once again exposed America's fractures. And of course, the COVID-19 pandemic left me and just about every other

American wondering if they'd ever again see friends, loved ones, or coworkers in person.

On the flipside, the lows of 2020 showed that BNC held more reason than ever to exist. Viewers of all races needed journalism that accurately showed people of color not as predators to fear, not as victims to pity, but as humans with joys, pains, realities, and dreams. Those under stay-at-home orders deserved to feel connected, no matter how isolated they were. Despite my initial qualms over having to anchor from home temporarily, the channel's goals fueled me to ditch my comfort zone, hook up a webcam, and learn what on Earth a VPN was.

Whether in our houses or other remote spots, my colleagues and I still covered the world. We looked into why COVID-19 was killing Black people at higher rates than other racial groups. We did Zoom calls with doctors who agreed that pre-existing conditions such as asthma, diabetes, high blood pressure, and obesity were all more prevalent in Black communities. We interviewed public health officials who attributed the underlying conditions and high mortality rates to limited health care access, especially in majority-Black neighborhoods. We showcased Black entrepreneurs who were building supermarkets, pharmacies, and urgent care centers in long-underserved areas, that way people wouldn't have to travel as far to get or stay healthy. I can only hope that raising these issues helped our viewers help themselves and their neighbors.

Working from home was cool and all, but the day I and others returned to a physical newsroom felt way better. I found calm in the pings of newswire alerts, the sound of mass typing and scribbling, and the rings of assignment desk phones. Because the pandemic was still going on, we were still at least six feet apart and wearing masks off-air, but those were small sacrifices. I was just glad my work pals were alive.

And there were more coworkers to greet. Because the stay-at-home directives had begun only about a month after BNC's launch, I still hadn't met much of the team.

But as it turned out, one young production staffer already knew who I was.

"I FaceTimed my dad the other day," she told me. "He smiled so big when I told him you're one of the anchors here. He says he loved watching you every night on CNN."

Then she unleashed the kicker.

"He says you were the first Black sports host he ever saw on national TV."

Her words took me aback. I tried thinking of Black hosts who had done nationally televised sports shows before my CNN debut in 1980. There'd been a handful of Black in-game analysts, but as far as actual hosts, I could only recall three: Irv Cross and Jayne Kennedy on CBS's *The NFL Today*, and Bryant Gumbel on NBC's *GrandStand*. It had taken me forty years to recognize my part in such a tiny club, one I had never set out to join. I just wanted to tell important stories, but if my roles helped people feel more represented and comfortable being themselves, spreading good however they saw fit, then I have lived my purpose.

I am so glad the club has grown. Black broadcasters are far more prominent on American television today than in the past, be it in sports or hard news. Better yet, they do incredible work.

Nonetheless, there will always be more work to do.

THE BLACK NEWS Channel experiment did not last. Despite reaching fifty million homes, ratings struggled. By March 2022, not even two rounds of layoffs could save the books. Its biggest investor pulled out. The office fell weeks behind on payroll. The company filed for bankruptcy. After just over two years of operation, the channel shut down.

The end of BNC doesn't diminish the good that my colleagues there did. They covered and uncovered truths at a time when facts had become vilified. They reported fairly without caving to false balance. They worked longer hours with fewer resources, which has sadly become a norm in America's newsrooms. They will always have my love.

As for this sixty-five-year-old, I felt like time had come to let the next class of broadcast storytellers take the reins. I wasn't sure where they would go next, but I knew their work would reward them.

On my way out of the office one last time, quietly to myself, I whispered my wish to them all. It sounded an awful lot like my old signoff phrase from *Inside the NBA*.

"As always, I'm Fred Hickman, hoping for God to bless. May all your jumpers hit nothing but the bottom of the net."

With Sheila and the kids.

15

'NEARER, MY GOD, TO THEE'

I HAVE SEEN THE END OF THE WORLD.

Okay, maybe not, but I have seen the one-minute video that the Cable News Network will air on loop when the moment comes. At one point, Ted Turner kept two copies of it: one in a bombproof lair in Tennessee, the other in a drawer in Atlanta. The running joke was that if the CNN control room didn't play it when the world ended, Ted would fire everyone. An intern leaked the footage onto the internet a few years back—and has hopefully been promoted since then. To any fiery and brimstoney viewers hoping that TV's closing seconds will be in high-definition, tough luck.

The video was recorded minutes before CNN's launch in 1980. It shows the U.S. Army, Navy, Marine, and Air Force marching bands standing in formation outside the channel's original headquarters. They play "Nearer, My God, to Thee," the very hymn the Titanic orchestra reportedly played as the ship sank. Rumor has it that Ted had requested "The Star-Spangled Banner" before deciding that it would've been too U.S.-centric for a global apocalypse.

That's all I know about this mortal realm's final chapter. I'll leave the rest to scientists who have actually studied this stuff.

As God knows, I've been wrong about endings before.

TAKE DETROIT, for example. I thought the city had been through with me since the day I left for drug rehab in 1986. Funny how liver cancer corrected me on that thirty-six years later.

I entered a pharmacy in early 2022, to pick up pills for my treatment. This was in Polk County, Florida, where I live now. The pharmacist told me he's from Detroit.

"You used to do sports on WDIV, right?" he asked.

I was shocked that anyone had recalled my time there. They weren't my proudest two years, but he seemed to think otherwise.

"We were so bummed when you left there," he added. "You were great!"

"I'm surprised you remember!" I told him. "Thank you very much. I appreciate that."

And I still appreciate it. His words didn't suddenly inspire me to move back to Five Mile Road—or relive any moments from my dark period—but hearing that I had brightened at least one Michigander's day back then gave me comfort.

He handed me just the medicine I needed.

I'M TAKING all kinds of medicines lately. Most of their names I can't spell or pronounce. One pill gives me an appetite; another takes it away. One makes my throat dry; another overproduces saliva. To beat the awful aftertastes as I swallow them each, I close my eyes and pretend they're chocolate chip cookies.

Walking distracts me from the side effects. I aim for a few thousand steps a day. Sometimes I make it. Sometimes I don't have energy to leave the house. I recharge by going to my lanai and looking toward Cape Canaveral. I figure watching a spacecraft soar miles into the air must at least count for something.

I also try to follow my late boss Bill MacPhail's prescriptions. He scribbled them down in one of his many notepads a long time ago. After Bill's death and the formation of CNN/SI, someone at Time Warner nailed a blown-up version of the handwritten wisdom onto a wall:

TAKE TIME TO:
THINK - It is the source of self-renewal
PLAY - It will keep you young
READ - It will rejuvenate you
WORSHIP - It is the acknowledgment of your limitations
HELP NEEDY PEOPLE - It will return more than
you give
SHOW LOVE - It is the key to life's greatest satisfactions
DAYDREAM - It will provide a roadmap for your future
LAUGH - It restores your balance

Bill was right. Wherever he is now, he still is.

Sheila helps me do all these things. We've been married for many years now, but nothing makes me smile in the morning like asking her, "Will you marry me?" I still ask her regularly. I don't care if I'm a cheeseball. The sound of her "yes" never gets old.

She is with me through every medical appointment. We pass time in the hospital by quoting the King James Bible. John 3:16. 2 Corinthians 3. Illness may rage inside me, but visualizing God-given armor—the "breastplate of righteousness" from Ephesians 6:14—comforts me.

I close my eyes and picture the holy site that is Wrigley Field. I imagine myself doing something I'd love to do there once in my life: lead a rendition of "Take Me Out to the Ball Game" during the seventh-inning stretch. In my dreams, I stand in the home announcers' booth, high above the checkerboard-patterned

Kentucky bluegrass, the wall of ivy, and the green clock with white dots instead of numbers. Flags wave in the breeze. No clouds in the blue sky. Everyone in the crowd—wherever they're from, however they look, even if they met only a minute ago—hugs and smiles as they sing. Jerry Pritikin, the stadium's famed "Bleacher Preacher," cheers me on. Maybe a kid over in Springfield is listening on the radio. I pump my fist . . . *"One! Two! Three!"* . . . and belt out the last note.

And the old ballgame continues.

AFTERWORD: 'LET'S TALK ABOUT FLYING'

HARRISON GOLDEN

Fred and I did our best bookwork over video chat. With him sitting on his lanai and me in my home office, we would jog memories, stumble upon factoids, flesh out scenes, and chisel prose. We would end our calls by brainstorming topics to write about next time. There was always a next time.

He looked up from his iPhone. He squinted toward the darkening Sunday sky. A small plane cruised above him.

He snapped his fingers. "How about this? Later this week, let's talk about flying."

Makes sense to me, Air Fred.

Aviation, after all, was a constant for him. The self-described son of "the best janitor that Capital Airport had ever seen" had grown up with planes surrounding him. As a CNN anchor, he had trekked tens of thousands of air miles a year for assignments. Looking out the window during all those long plane rides had inspired him to get his private pilot license. By the time of his cancer diagnosis, he hadn't manned an aircraft in years, but he hoped to again once he reached remission.

"After I'm through with this battle, maybe I'll get back up there."

The battle ended that Wednesday morning. Fredrick Douglas Hickman was gone. He had spent months on his autobiography without seeing it published.

But in the hours and days following his death, my friend received many assists. Tributes picked up where the manuscript had left off. Filling newsprint, web space, and airtime were accounts of the lives he had touched, whether he knew it or not.

"When you see charisma, you know it, and Fred Hickman had charisma," CNN and ESPN alum Dan Patrick said on his radio show that Thursday. "He had that twinkle in his eye. He had a little bit of mischief in him."

A *New York Times* obituary recognized Fred as "one of the first Black people to anchor a national cable sportscast" and an "insightful interviewer who carved a place for sports at CNN." The article quoted former *Sports Tonight* coanchor Vince Cellini: "Fred was the most naturally talented person I've ever worked with on television. He had an electricity that jumped through the screen."

On the social media platform then known as Twitter, former CNN sports reporter Dan Hicks recalled the dozens who had worked at *Sports Tonight* under Bill MacPhail: "Bill always said Fred was the most talented. And he was right."

Viewers agreed. They eulogized the man whose style had led them to watch CNN past their bedtimes. Referring to Fred's longtime partnership with Nick Charles, *Boston Globe* columnist Chad Finn wrote, "I'll always remember him as an affable half of the best tandem of sports hosts I've ever had the good fortune to watch." "What I'd give to grab the old cable box right before bed, unspool its cord across the living room to the couch, punch on CNN, and watch Hick and Nick," wrote *Tulsa World* columnist Guerin Emig. Joe Scarborough, host of cable TV's *Morning Joe*: "Hard to explain the magic of Fred Hickman and Nick Charles on CNN's *Sports Tonight* in the 1980s. . . . The program's pacing was pitch perfect. Revolutionary." And San Francisco TV reporter Will Tran: "If cool was a person, it would be Fred Hickman."

People of color who had watched Fred honored him as a pathmaker. "He was an excellent broadcaster whose legacy paved the way for Stuart Scott, Michael Wilbon, Stan Verrett, Steve Wyche, Jim Trotter, Jemele Hill, and others," Kyle T. Mosley wrote on *Sports Illustrated's* HBCU blog. ESPN's Mark Jones tweeted: "Fred inspired countless Black men on the come-up. He made the dream a reality to us with his smooth voice and culture vibes." Fox Sports studio host Mike Hill said that "long before I was inspired by any sports anchor on *SportsCenter*, Fred was the anchor I looked up to. He was solid, great, and looked like ME. A rarity back then." Former NBA star and *Inside the NBA* panelist Kenny Smith acknowledged him as "the first that allowed his ethnicity to show easily and comfortably." To *Entertainment Tonight* host Kevin Frazier, Fred "was the blueprint I followed."

Others recalled his off-air generosity. "Fred was such a welcoming presence . . . always with a laugh, a quip, or a story," said Hannah Storm, who had worked with Fred at both CNN and ESPN. Longtime New York Yankees radio announcer Suzyn Waldman: "No matter what was thrown at him, he'd smile, handle it, and make us all better. He was also the kindest man I've ever met." Jeanne Burns, Fred's coanchor at WVLA-TV in Baton Rouge, wrote on Facebook, "The day I met Fred Hickman . . . I instantly felt like we had known each other for a lifetime."

Similar feelings spanned office hierarchies. "He was so cool with us low-level grunts when he didn't have to be," said former CNN intern Kevin Noon. Studio host Bob Lorenz, who had worked with Fred at CNN and the YES Network, said this: "It didn't matter if you were a high-level executive or a production assistant on your first day. Fred made you feel special as soon as he met you." Tasmin Mahfuz, who had anchored with Fred at Maryland TV station WDVM in 2018 and 2019, said on air that "he cared about everyone in the building." NBC anchor Willie Geist, who had started his TV career as a production assistant at CNN/SI, wrote on Twitter, "I studied his moves—his joy for work, his respect for colleagues—and hoped I could be like him someday. Thank you for showing how it's done, Fred."

Springfield, Illinois, gave thanks as well. Governor J. B. Pritzker called Fred "trailblazing." A *State Journal-Register* article called him "groundbreaking" and quoted his high school history teacher, Sue Davies-Yoggerst, with whom he had stayed in touch until the end: "He never got a big head about being famous or important. I was just so proud of Fred." Early the following year, Illinois lawmakers would adopt a resolution in Fred's memory:

> Resolved, by the Senate of the 102nd General Assembly of the State of Illinois, that we mourn the passing of Fred Hickman and extend our sincere condolences to his family, friends, and all who knew and loved him.

Even Shaquille O'Neal shared nice words. The legend, who had famously fallen one Fred-vote short of being the NBA's first unanimous Most Valuable Player, confirmed that he had put past disagreements to bed. "Fred was always nice to me. . . . Forget all that stuff," he said during a memorial segment on *Inside the NBA*. "There's nothing more precious than life. We'll never see another guy like Fred again."

Yet for all that praise, there were still more gems. And I didn't have to look far.

Mack Hickman has Fred stories. About the broadcaster who called suburban Atlanta high school football games in his spare time. About the neighbor who bought hundreds of dollars in gear for a varsity wrestler who couldn't afford it. About the Christian who, at his last Thanksgiving dinner, spent more time praying than eating.

Mack told me about his father's final hours: "He had gone to the hospital for pain in his stomach. By this point, doctors couldn't do much aside from making him comfortable. He said, 'Before I pass away, before they give me anything that will knock me out, I need to have communion.'"

So communion Fred received. A few minutes after a nurse told Mack that his dad likely wouldn't make it past noon, the chaplain approached the bed. "He prayed over my father, my stepmother, my sister, and me," Mack said. "The chaplain said a Bible verse that my dad had told me since I was little: Psalms 23:4. For me growing up, this was the quintessential verse. My father always recited the King James Version. And there the chaplain was, picking that line over all others: 'Yea, though I walk through the valley of the shadow of death, I will fear no evil: for thou art with me; thy rod and thy staff they comfort me.'

"I was next to my stepmom. She and I were crying. She whispered into my father's ear, 'You can let go now, Fred. You can let go.'

"As soon as she whispered that, his machine started beeping. The blood pressure started dropping. Seconds later, that was it.

"I do Muay Thai and jiu jitsu and have been in the U.S. Army for almost a decade, but what my father did then was the greatest display of toughness I've ever seen. He had wanted to make sure he was right with God first, and he did it. He acknowledged that the last prayer he was going to hear had been said. That's the example of faith I'll be thinking about for the rest of my life."

Somewhere along the way, Fred Hickman taught his son about flying.

SEE YOU AGAIN: A POEM

GABRIELLE ELIZABETH HICKMAN

If I said I was cold, you would move the sun closer
    so I could get warm.
"To the moon and back" was not just a saying, you
    meant every word.
You have taught me what unwavering love has
    been since I was brought into this world.
Never faulting, not even on the day you were met
    with those heavenly gates.
I am jealous that every angel gets to see you smile
    and laugh every day.
All the more while being my happiest knowing
    you are surrounded by everything perfect,
    everything good, and everything you deserve.

This is to my guardian angel.
You have done everything and more in your time
    on this Earth.
Touching everyone with light and love everywhere
    you turned.

With every step you took, you made the deepest
    footprint,
Leaving a permanent mark in everyone's heart.
With every tear that has fallen from my eyes,
It has been mixed with everything joyful and
    somber.
God gifted me with you in this life and the next.
For that, I will always be grateful.
This is not forever, and I know we will meet again.
When we do, promise me one thing.
That I will be greeted with an enormous hug,
    wrapped in your warmth
And comfort at those pearly gates.

<u>ACKNOWLEDGMENTS</u>

The making of this book has brought out the generosity in so many people, starting with Fred himself. He could have picked anyone, but the fact that someone who had lived such a colorful life would entrust me with even his most candid stories is a responsibility that I will always uphold. I only wish he could hold a copy.

Fred's surviving wife and children deserve their own thanks. Writing any book (let alone an autobiography) can feel gruelingly all-encompassing for anyone (let alone someone fighting terminal cancer), but Sheila, Mack, and Gabby each gave Fred the time, headspace, and reassurance to do so on his own terms. In Fred's absence, the words and images they provided have turned this final product into a portable time capsule of a life well lived.

Cory Charles's enthusiasm has been another blessing. As the surviving wife of Nick Charles, she wasted no time in dusting off old photographs of the *Sports Tonight* duo. Having spent a quarter-century at CNN in her own right, she secured additional elements and encouragement from others who knew, worked with, and loved Fred.

Additional recognition goes to two men whose advocacy allowed me and Fred to work together: former Baton Rouge news director Gary Wordlaw and talent agent John Butte.

And to the light of my life, librarian Brittany O'Neill, with whom spreading the joy of words is a team sport: I love being on your team.

Harrison Golden

ILLUSTRATION CREDITS

All but the following images appear courtesy of the Hickman family:

16 — Fred working for WICS: Terry Young/Marvin Scattergood
24 — Fred in a Cubs hat, Nick in a White Sox hat: Cory Charles
42 — Fred in a CNN makeup room: Rhonda Barrymore
48 — Fred on the CNN/SI set: Steve Stahl
48 — Fred and Nick at a podium: Cory Charles
70 — A papier-mâché Fred Hickman: Brian Tees
70 — Fred at YES with former CNN/SI coworkers: Brian Tees

Fred Hickman spent nearly twenty years anchoring *Sports Tonight*, a nightly sports news show that premiered shortly after CNN's launch in 1980. His half-century in broadcasting also included time on TNT's *Inside the NBA*, Turner Sports' Winter Olympics and Goodwill Games coverage, ESPN's *SportsCenter*, the YES Network, Fox Sports South, and the Black News Channel. He earned two CableACE awards and a New York Sports Emmy. Upon Hickman's death in 2022, the National Association of Black Journalists honored him as a "shining example of perseverance and an incredible role model for Black journalists."

Harrison Golden writes for the Society for American Baseball Research. He has worked as a producer for Fox News in New York and as an NBC affiliate reporter in Louisiana. He has contributed work to CNN.com, *USA Today*, and *Interview*. He currently lives in North Carolina.